Weeke

C000179289

THE
YORKSHIRE
DALES

Weekend Walks

THE YORKSHIRE DALES

Anthony Burton

Photographs by Mike Williams

AURUM PRESS

First published in Great Britain 2000
by Aurum Press Ltd
25 Bedford Avenue, London WC1B 3AT

Copyright © 2000 by Anthony Burton

Photographs copyright © 2000 by Mike Williams

Maps reproduced from Ordnance Survey 1:25 000 Pathfinder, Outdoor Leisure
and Explorer map series with the permission of The Controller of Her Majesty's
Stationery Office © Crown copyright: Licence No: 43453U

A catalogue record for this book is available from the British Library.

ISBN 1 85410 675 9

Designed by Robert Updegraff
Printed and bound in Italy
by Printers Srl, Trento

Cover Ingleborough as seen from the Whernside walk
Title Page the view out over Horton Moor from Pen-y-ghent

Contents

Attermire Scar on the Kirkby Fell walk from Malham. The numerous caves in the rocks served as homes for Ice Age residents.

Introduction

The seven walking centres are all situated within the boundaries of the Yorkshire Dales National Park and have been selected principally because excellent walks are available in the countryside around them, but also because they are attractive places in their own right with reasonable facilities and somewhere to get food and slake the thirst at the end of the day. Two walks are described from each centre, starting wherever possible, from the town or village itself or from very close by. Most visitors these days arrive by car, and the hope is that the vehicle will not be needed again until it is time to go home at the end of an enjoyable weekend's walking. The walks themselves are all between 10 and 15 miles (16 and 24 km) long and should provide a good, but not over demanding, day's walk. Those who are taking a longer time in the area will find that by using the recommended centres, they can enjoy every aspect of the region – and for the really energetic, it adds up to two very full weeks.

Inexperienced walkers sometimes have doubts about how long a particular walk might take. A useful guide is Nasmith's rule which suggests a walking rate of 4 km per hour on the flat, with 4 minutes added for every 30 metres climbed. So, for example, Walk 1 from Horton is 20km long which would call for a walking time of 5 hours. But it includes a climb to the highest point in the Dales, the summit of Ingleborough which is roughly 560 metres above the start, which means you need to add an extra hour and a quarter. So a realistic time for the whole outing would be around seven hours to allow for stops along the way. It should be stressed that this is only an average. Some walkers will make slower progress, stopping regularly to admire the scenery or for a closer inspection of some point of interest; others will put their heads down and press on all day at a brisk pace. As the author who devised and tested all these routes, all I can say is that I personally enjoyed every one of them and found each to be a reasonable and comfortable day's outing. I hope that the reader and walker will share my enthusiasm and as a native Yorkshireman, I hope that at the end you will agree with me that the Dales have a beauty and majesty all of their own.

THE DALES

Anyone walking in the Dales soon realises that there are two very different landscapes associated with two very different rocks – the limestone, sullen and grey on wet days, but gleaming white in the sun, and the dark, squared blocks of millstone grit. The boundary between the two can be quite precise: on the walk over Kirkby Fell out of Malham, for example, you look to one side of the path and all you see is gritstone, look to the other side and limestone is just as dominant. And the presence of the two rocks will mean real differences in the land around them. This may come as a bit of a surprise, because if you view the area as a whole, on a relief map for example, it looks remarkably homogenous, like an oversized sheet of paper crumpled by a giant hand, the folded hills criss-crossed by valleys. The story begins some 300 million years ago in the Carboniferous Period.

Warm, shallow seas washed over the land, home to countless millions of sea creatures. As they died, their flesh rotted away and bones and shells settled on the sea floor. Age after age rolled on and, as more matter fell, so it created ever more pressure compacting the tiny marine creatures to form rocks and reefs which eventually became a vast slab of limestone 820 feet (250 metres) thick, covering the whole region. The sea still washed the area, advancing and retreating, depositing mud and sand on top of the limestone to create shales and sandstones. It all sounds simple enough, but over the millions of years there were local variations. From these basic forms all our modern landscape developed, but it was given its final shape much more recently – practically yesterday when viewed over the aeons of geological time. The crucial event was the last great Ice Age, a mere 20,000 years ago. Everywhere you can see what the ice has done. Look up to the head of any dale, and it is not hard to imagine the glacier moving inexorably onward, wearing out a great scoop in the land. The ice attacked the main limestone sheet on the heights, wearing away everything above it, cracking and fissuring it into the typical limestone pavements, most spectacularly above Malham Cove. Sometimes, the glacier rolled boulders along in its path, then abandoned them perched on high as you can see on the approach to Whernside.

The ice worked in different ways on different rocks, eroding them at varying rates. The resulting sandwich broke down into ledges as they were later eroded by water, creating waterfalls such as those at Aysgarth.. The sandstone and shales survived on the tops of the higher hills, giving the distinctive piled up plateau, such as that of Ingleborough. Difference in weathering produced the distinctive features of the region. The water that pours down from the hard gritstone can disappear when it reaches the fissures in the limestone, creating pot holes, such as Hull Pot and Gaping Gill, the water in the latter case reappearing only after creating the vast spaces of Ingleborough Cave. It often seems that limestone dominates everything, if only because it is constantly breaking through its thin covering of soil in little outcrops and longer escarpments, while its light colour adds to its prominence. The darker gritstone wears down much more slowly, producing the more rounded hills. And the differences do not end there. One of the delights of the limestone uplands is the short, springy turf which is full of grasses such as sheep's fescue and dotted with harebells and wild thyme. Walking is easy, a bouncy pleasure. Turn to the gritstone, however, and the picture changes. Here you find peat moorland, with its typical cover of reedy grasses and rough tussocks, sphagnum moss and snowy-headed cotton grass. When rain falls on the limestone, it quickly drains down through the turf and disappears through the fissures. On the moors, it collects above the rock and is held by the mosses. Those who walk the moorland paths soon become aware what that means as they encounter the dark, treacly pools and squelchy, black peat – a straight line path on the map can become a series of zig-zags round the oozy bogs. The reward is there, however, in some of the wildest scenery the Dales can offer, which gives the walk over Plover Hill and Pen-y-ghent, for example, its splendid character – but there is a price to be paid.

Natural forces may have created the fundamentals of the landscape, but man has had as powerful an influence. There is, however, very little evidence of man's earliest settlements in the region. On Walk 2 from Malham, the craggy hillside of Attermire Scar looks about the most inhospitable place you could imagine, but at the very end of the last Ice Age, the caves up here made a welcome shelter – and what a different world it was. The bones found here include woolly rhino and bear and in among them reindeer antlers carved and decorated with patterns by the men who came here more than 10,000 years ago. After that we have to move on in time another 8000 years to find evidence of a ritual site, a typical henge monument of the New Stone Age. You can visit this on the second Aysgarth walk, but do not expect another Stonehenge. This is just a slightly oval enclosure, defined by bank and ditch. Travelling on again to the Bronze Age it seems that, if there was any settlement in the area, then little has survived to show it. The Celtic tribes of the Iron Age, however, found at least one of the hills to their liking, and circled the high plateau of Ingleborough with a great defensive wall of gritstone boulders. From such forts they could look down on the Roman army who were if anything even less enthusiastic about the bleak uplands. They did, however, start to exploit the veins of lead ore and, as Romans always did, they built their roads, one of which forms part of Walk 2 from Hawes, running from the fort of Virosidum at modern Bainbridge. But from all those thousands of years of human occupation, we see only the merest traces left on the land.

It was only after the Romans left that the real change that we can still see today arrived in the Dales. In popular legend, the Norsemen were fearsome warriors whose favourite activities were rape, pillage, slaughter and general mayhem. Not here: they came as settlers and they stayed. They have left us many of the common names of the region: beck, crag, tarn and even dale itself all come from the Norse. They established villages with central enclosures where stock were herded in for the night, and which survive as the greens which are still to be seen in so many villages today. They raised sheep and cattle which roamed the hills in summer and were brought down to the valleys for winter feed, establishing a pattern that also survives. It was a system which remained unchanged until the Norman invasion which brought two new powerful forces to the land – the feudal lord and the church. Something of the power of the Norman lord can be gauged from the splendid fortress of Bolton Castle, which totally dominates much of Wensleydale and the surrounding area. None of the great monasteries are encountered on any of the walks, but their influence was widely felt. The monks of Fountains Abbey owned vast flocks of sheep which roamed over immense areas, hence the name Fountains Fell for the hills above Malham Tarn. The main farm, or grange, was linked back to the Abbey by Mastiles Lane, which you follow for a little way on Walk 1 from Malham.

The dissolution of the monasteries by Henry VIII was the prelude to a period of rapid change. The vast abbey holdings were broken up and sold off. A new generation of farmers grew up, owning their own land and with a real incentive to make improvements. They began to make better use of the land and they prospered, and expressed their new confidence in solid, stone houses built to last. You can see them in every Dale village with their stone mullioned windows, roofs of heavy stone slabs and inscriptions, many from the seventeenth century, over the doors. More importantly, these farmers no longer had the same access to virtually unlimited tracts of land, so there was a need to husband resources and establish fixed boundaries. There was still room for stock to roam in the summer, but winter feed presented quite a new problem – and the solution created the unique landscape that we see today.

It is a broad generalisation, but largely true, that the nearer to the valley floor you go, the richer the land – and the more valuable. So the fertile valley was divided up into quite small units which had to be made as efficient as possible. The hay meadows are among the glories of the Dales, rich and lush, with a profusion of wild flowers and herbs, often tinged yellow, not with the ubiquitous gaudy rape of other areas, but subtly coloured by buttercup, globe flower and birdsfoot trefoil, in among which are the different grasses, clovers and even delicately tinted orchids. Dotted throughout the fields are the square, stone barns. As hay was harvested it was stored in the loft ready for winter, when the cattle were brought into the byres on the ground floor. The hay was forked down to the beasts, and the muck shovelled out and spread over the fields to enrich the land and begin the cycle all over again. It was, and is, a very efficient system and persists today, though much reduced. Every dale shows it – the small, inner hay fields, the larger fields of rough pasture up the slopes and the wilder uplands, all defined by complex patterns of stone walls. One of the best places to see the change is around Malham where the newer system stands alongside the strips of the medieval farmers, and in Malham itself one of the old field barns has been preserved to show just how the system worked. Although sheep farming is the predominant feature – and all walkers should be grateful for those four-legged lawnmowers that keep the upland turf in such excellent condition – cattle farming is also an important part of the economy. The broader valleys, notably Wensleydale, are particularly good for dairy herds, hence the famous cheese, still made in Hawes.

One of the great question marks hanging over the Dales today is just how long this unique landscape can be preserved. It is unquestionably cheaper to drive in posts and string wire than it is to go through the complex, laborious and skilful process of build-

A crazy-paving pattern of fields in Swaledale, seen from the path above Muker.

ing stone walls. Rolling up the hay into great roly-poly puddings and encasing it in plastic - and the new versions are a startling lime green - is simple and efficient. Why bother with the old style hay meadows, when fertilisers, pesticides, insecticides and several other -cides can produce just the grass you want with no waste? Hill farmers are not wealthy. Next time you exclaim over the price of a leg of English lamb in the supermarket, consider the fact that the farmer was lucky if he got half that sum for the entire beast. Fortunately, the National Park authorities are aware of the problem, and accept that if the rest of us want to preserve the beauties and character of the region, then someone has to pay. So there are financial incentives, all aimed at conservation in partnership with the farming community.

The hill farm seems to define the Dales, but other forces have had an impact. Industry too has touched the area. Quarrying and lead mining have both left their marks on the land, the former still very active and particularly noticeable on the slopes above Ribblesdale. Lead mining may have ended but the scars remain, and there is a particularly good opportunity to explore the history of the industry on Walk 2 from Kettlewell. You can peer down deep shafts and look down the long drainage adits, wander among the spoil heaps and surface buildings and look up the hill to a tall chimney, which looks quite incongruous in such a wild setting. Lead smelting was not a healthy business, and certainly no one would want the fumes settling down on a village street and, just as importantly for the entrepreneur, the ore was expensive to transport. From the late eighteenth century, the ore was crushed and heated in a cupola near the site and then the vapours were passed through long flues where they sublimated, depositing the metal from the gases. The exhaust fumes eventually emerged from the chimney to be dispersed by the moorland winds. Textile mills appear here and there, but never packed together as in other parts of Yorkshire, but there are examples met along the way at Aysgarth, Gayle and Malham.

The natural history of the area is every bit as rich and varied as the human variety. Some indication of the variety of plant life has already been given. Woodland does not feature to a very great extent on these walks, but trees are still a very important part of the landscape. Ash, sycamore and elder predominate, but one of the more unusual features is to be found on the limestone pavements. The grikes, the fissures in the rock, support a number of plants from hart's tongue fern to the delicate wood anemone, but also provide a refuge where hawthorn can become established without the voracious sheep attacking the young shoots. So one finds trees, bent and twisted by the wind, but still surviving, springing it seems right out of bare rock.

No one walking the area can be unaware of the bird life, and nothing seems better to epitomise the loneliness of the uplands than the curlew. Seemingly untroubled by human presence, the birds will often come quite close, peering at the human invaders of their domain before wheeling off with their long, drawn out cry with its questioning lift. The other cry heard almost as often is that of the lapwing, which in this area takes its name from the call, a drawling 'tewit'. The meadow pipit's sweet little song is common, but that other upland songster, the skylark, seems to have all but disappeared – not once was that song heard on any of the walks. The valleys have their own residents, and one of the most attractive has to be the oyster catcher with its handsome black and white plumage set off by orange beak and rather fetching pink legs. Dippers, herons and, with luck, kingfishers can all be seen at the water's edge while sand martins and swallows give aerobatic displays overhead. All these and others are welcome sights, but one bird is always likely to make you all but jump out of your skin. The grouse crouches down in the long grass and heather of the moor until you are right on top of it, when it starts up in your face with a furious whirr of wings. One can hardly blame the grouse scaring us considering what we do to it, as the many shooting butts on the moor testify. Finally, from 1999 onwards there is a possibility of seeing a bird of prey which had completely vanished from the Dales. The red kite has been reintroduced, and now ornithologists are waiting to see if the various pairs will breed.

Animals are never far away, though mostly in the form of sheep and cattle, including the traditional small, black cows of the area. Rabbit populations, which were severely depleted by myxomatosis not so very long ago, seem to have made a full recovery and there are few walks where you do not meet them along the way. They have one important natural enemy to contend with, the stoat, and there is a fair chance of spotting this sinuous little beast – there were three sightings during the fourteen walks for this book, not a bad ratio. Otters are to be found in the rivers, but here alas no sightings can be recorded, no doubt a longer, more patient waterside vigil is needed. No one can expect to see everything on a short visit, but anyone walking the area who delights in the natural world will not come away disappointed.

The walking itself has great variety, but it is in the nature of the landscape that, even if one wanted to do so, there is very little chance of creating interesting circular walks that do not involve going up into the hills. For the majority who visit the Dales, this is an attraction rather than a disadvantage, and none of the hills, however grand they may look, qualifies as an actual mountain – even Ingleborough, grandest of them all, stops short of the magical figure of 3000 feet. On the whole, the climbs are not too demanding even if some, notably Pen-y-ghent, involve a certain amount of scrambling over rocks near the summit. A more demanding problem is posed by the peat moorland – and Pen-y-ghent manages to include a good deal of that as well as a rock escarpment, while Buckden Pike can claim to be the ooziest of the lot. Conditions vary with the weather and obviously the wetter the weather, the boggier the ground will become. Even limestone gets a little more difficult in the wet as the rock becomes slippery. Bad weather also brings a problem familiar to all hill walkers – cloud sitting over the tops. There is little pleasure to be had from climbing into the grey. There will be no views to enjoy and the cloud will probably have rain inside it, even if it is fine down below. On such days, it is the sensible option to go for a walk at a lower level. Fortunately, it is always possible to assess the situation from the valley floor, but it still makes sense to check the local forecast to make sure there are no nasty surprises hurrying towards you.

The walks in this book fall within the National Park, which means that on the whole they are well signposted, and stiles and gates are in good repair. The more popular routes, particularly up the Three Peaks and along the Pennine Way, have often been paved with rough stone blocks to ease the passage over the worst of the bogs and to counteract erosion. The Dales Way, which also passes through the region is arguably more attractive than the Pennine Way, but is less well used and suffers a good deal less from the passage of boots. Nevertheless, there is some genuinely rough, wild country in the Dales and walkers must be prepared for it. Walking boots are more or less essential, especially for the peat moors. Genuine waterproof clothing should always be carried – one walker who was met along the way seemed to think an umbrella was good protection until a gale force gust on Ingleborough nearly resulted in an inadvertent lesson in paragliding. You will see that several of the walks stay in open country, with no facilities for refreshments, so you need to take your own food and, much more importantly, drink. Safety is always a factor on long walks, and there is an added risk here. The limestone is honeycombed with cracks, fissures, pot holes and caves, many of which offer a chance of exploration. But those who want to enter the underground world should either visit one of the show caves or make arrangements to join experienced and properly equipped cavers. Impromptu investigation of holes in the ground is to be very much discouraged.

Perhaps the most common cause of a ruined day out is getting lost. Every effort has been made to ensure that the instructions in this book are as clear as possible, but fog, mist and cloud can render some of them all but useless. A direction to head for a particular barn or tree, let alone a distant hill is little use when all you can see is an unrecognisable shape virtually lost in enveloping grey. It happens to everyone sooner or later, and in these circumstances the only reliable guides are map and compass. It is astonishing how easy it is to lose all sense of direction when visibility is reduced to a few metres, and how frustrating it can be to look for something as simple as the next stile in a long wall. The compass is then not just helpful but essential.

Hazards and problems need to be mentioned, but only because they can be overcome with just a little planning and by following the elementary rules; check the weather, be properly equipped and if you are walking alone make sure someone knows where you are going and when you expect to return. Different seasons require different precautions. In winter, for example, overhanging snow cornices on the brows of hills have to be avoided and paths will no longer be visible under snow. But it can be a glorious season, and there is no reason why walking in the Dales cannot be an all year experience. As someone who has walked here since school days, I look back on winter walks with at least as much pleasure as those of bright summer days. So whenever you choose to go, enjoy the walks in safety and the best that I can wish is that by the end you will share my enthusiasm for this most beautiful area.

Malham

Not surprisingly, this is one of the most popular centres in the Dales. It is a beautiful little village and very close to two of the most dramatic features in the whole region, both of which are visited on the first walk.

WALK 1 | Gordale Scar, Darnbrook and Malham Cove

11 miles (17.5 km) via Gordale Scar 12.5 miles (20km) using detour
See maps on pages 24 and 25

The spectacular formations of Gordale Scar and Malham Cove nature reserve and the wild country at the head of Airedale are all visited. The longer route is offered for those who, for whatever reason, do not fancy the clamber up by the falls in the gorge.

The walk starts by taking the road opposite the Buck Inn **1**, passing the Youth Hostel and signposted to Gordale. Cross the river by the little green, very popular with sun bathing mallard, and continue on past the farm where all the barns have been converted to housing. After a while, the great gash in the hillside that is Gordale Scar comes into view, while over to the right **A** you can see strip lynchets, the terraced fields created by medieval farmers. Cross over the bridge **2** and where the road bends right continue on the obvious path to the ravine. The nearer you get, the more daunting it seems as sheer cliffs seem to block the way ahead. Then the gully turns and you can see the lower falls with rocks to either side **B**. There is a direct route up Gordale Scar which goes to the left of the waterfall, and well worn and polished rocks show where countless numbers of walkers have made the journey, but it does involve a little rough scrambling. If you do not wish to take this route – and in wet weather the rock can be slippery and obviously will be even worse in winter ice and snow – turn to the next paragraph for the alternative route. The short climb up by the falls brings you to the heart of the gorge, a magnificent sight with a second set of falls cascading between the sheer walls. The water falls through a ring of rock, where once it had disappeared underground. Now the going is very much easier and as you emerge from the depths you take the

clear path swinging away to the left and running round the limestone outcrops. At the road **3** you turn slightly to the right along
the footpath to a junction with the track coming in from the right
6. The two routes are now reunited, and the description of the rest
of the walk continues after the next paragraph.

Those not taking the direct route – but whatever you do, make
sure you walk up to the first falls anyway, it is a sight not to be missed
– should now return to the road at **2**. Turn left up the road, which
climbs quite steeply and gives you an even better view of the strip
lynchets, before it arrives at a much wilder landscape, where stone
glints from hilltops. Where the road ends **4** turn left onto the path
with the wall to the left to continue the steady climb up through
what is now typically knobbly limestone country. Eventually reaching the top of the hill **5** you turn left onto the track beside the wall.
You are now on Mastiles Lane, the main route in medieval times
from Fountains Abbey to Fountains Fell. Others came this way
before the monks, for you will walk across the now scarcely visible
low banks of what was a Roman camp **C**. This is most enjoyable
walking over open grassland beside a rutted track, with a softly ser-
rated margin of hills as a backdrop. Cross the stream that is soon to
plunge down Gordale Scar and join the direct route at the road **6**.

At this point, those who have taken the direct route continue
straight ahead, the rest turn right. The route is clearly signposted as
a bridleway to Middle House. This is also the farm approach road,
and soon Malham Tarn comes into view with its fringe of woodland backed by dark crags. From a distance the farm looks impossi-
bly remote, but as you get closer you can see what a good situation
it enjoys, set in a little craggy bowl and surrounded by surprisingly
lush fields. Where the approach road begins to swing right towards
the farm **7** carry straight on up the grassy hillside to the ladder stile
and gate on the skyline. Now you are getting into splendid, rough
upland country, walking on a path that strikes through a fractured
landscape of rocky outcrops.

At the top of the hill, continue on the stony path with the wall to
the right that takes you round the knoll. This is real lumpy limestone
country, of soft turf, with knobbles of stone breaking through below
the long escarpment edge. It is a great playground for young rabbits,
chasing each other around the rocks. Where tracks divide **8** take the
green path to the left, signposted to Darnbrook, passing to the left
of Middle House Hill. This is upland walking at its best, for although
the scenery may be wild, the walking is as comfortable as can be on

The dry valley above Malham Cove.

the springy turf. Crossing a stone stile by a gate, you now look down on a broad green track leading into the next valley. The descent gradually steepens, following the line of a gully to the left until eventually you reach a footbridge at the confluence of two streams, which meet at the end of this beautiful valley. Cross a ladder stile and take the path across the fields heading for the isolated barn to the left of the main farm buildings. The house itself is a fine example of the old vernacular, with dripstone mouldings over its mullioned windows.

Leave the field by the gate **9** and turn left onto the road. You have now reached the watershed between Littondale, running towards Wharfedale, and Airedale where you began, and this lonely moorland road is now heading back towards the latter. Stay with the road for a mile (1.5 km) to a point where it turns left, the wall on the left ends and an obvious track cuts across the road **10**. Turn left, and you are now joining the Pennine Way. For such a well-used route this section is surprisingly ill-defined on the ground. Cross the field at an angle to the road to a stile by the gate and continue up the hillock to the isolated corner of walls on the right. Turn right to follow the line of the wall to a ladder stile by a prominent, isolated tree. Now the way becomes much clearer as you head down the shallow valley with the wall to your right and low, rounded hills to either side.

At the foot of the hill **11** turn left onto the wide forest road heading into the National Trust nature reserve. You soon get glimpses of the waters of Malham Tarn gleaming through the trees, and there is a chance to turn off to the right to reach a hide for watching the bird life on and around the lake. Meanwhile the walk takes you up through interesting mixed woodland, where more exotic conifers rub branches with native trees. It becomes increasingly craggy and a narrow passage through the rocks, blasted away like a railway cutting, brings you to the imposing verandah of Malham Tarn House **D**, now a field studies centre. The path slides away unobtrusively behind the building with its grand view and private boat houses, to emerge from the woods near the water's edge. There is no shortage of wildfowl here, including coots, superficially similar to the more common moorhen, but easily recognisable by their disappearing act as they dive beneath the water, staying submerged for several seconds as they feed.

Where the track goes through a gate **12** and begins to turn away from the tarn, turn right onto the grassy track beside the water, staying with the Pennine Way. This brings you down to the road **13** where you turn right to cross the stream debouching from the tarn. Cross over the cattle grid and turn left to follow the path, which veers off left towards a wall. On reaching the wall turn right to arrive at a dry valley, a splendid place of limestone cliffs and caves that emerges very dramatically above a deep ravine. Turn sharp left for a steep descent on the stony path beside the brooding gully. After that a surprisingly flat path leads forward to the best known

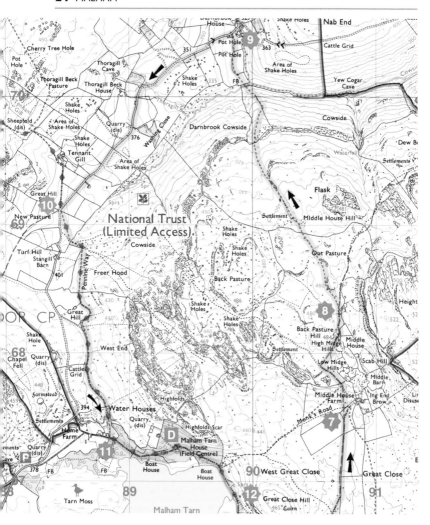

of the limestone pavements marking the top of Malham Cove **E**. Deep fissures run through the stone, so that progress is a bit like playing hopscotch over the rocks. It stretches for about 980 feet (300 metres) and on the left it falls away to a sheer 305 feet (80 metres) high cliff. Formed in the Ice Age along the line of the Craven Fault, it once had what must have been a spectacular waterfall cascading down the face, but the water has long since found an underground passage, emerging near the foot of the cliff to form the headwaters of the River Aire.

This is a very popular tourist attraction, and the way up and down beside the cliff face has been eased by the creation of a staircase of rough stone blocks. At the bottom follow the obvious path beside the little stream and head back towards Malham. Turn left at the road, passing the little field barn, restored by the National Trust **F**. It is worth the pause before returning to the centre and other, probably liquid, attractions.

WALK 2
Kirkby Fell and Kirkby Malham
12 miles (19.5 km) See map on pages 30 and 31

An invigorating walk across the hills that separate Airedale from Ribblesdale, with a gentler return which includes a visit to a high waterfall and to the delightful village of Kirkby Malham.

The walk again starts at the Buck Inn, but this time turn up the road to Langcliffe and Malham Tarn, passing the telephone box. Just opposite Beck Hall **1** turn left up the bridleway and left again on reaching the broad track, which almost immediately divides and you follow it round to the right. From here you get a good view of Malham Cove and the intricate pattern of fields that surrounds it, and one cannot help wondering how such strange shapes evolved. There is a gentle climb to a track junction where you turn left to face the archetypal Dales landscape of small irregular fields, liberally spattered with field barns.

Immediately after crossing the stream, leave the track by crossing the ladder stile on the right **2**. Head across the stream to the gateway by the barn, then turn away from the wall to head for the patch of limestone at the top of the hillock. Cross the stile by the gate and continue to head for the small gap in the hills, keeping the stream on your left. You finally cross the now tiny stream and continue uphill with the wall on the right to end the first stage of the climb up from Malham. Looking back there is a fine view of the village and the surrounding country with the whole pattern of the land laid out in front of you. The bright green of the hay meadows positively shines out, with one fertile strip rising like a grass ladder with stone walls for rungs, up the hillside. Now the way meanders through a jumble of humps and hollows **A**, the grassed over spoil heaps of old mine workings, with the occasional splodge of yellow paint or arrow to reassure you that you are still on track.. The miners knew that the minerals were to be found along fault lines, and there could be no clearer indication than here, where it is all limestone to the right of the path, all gritstone to the left. Crossing a ladder stile, continue up a hillside teeming with rabbits. The path now swings to the right, where walkers have kicked their own mini-staircase into the turf of the hillside.

Having at last reached the top of the climb almost 1000 feet (305 metres) above Malham, you arrive at a wide expanse of reedy moorland with a view of the hunched bulk of Pen-y-ghent through the gap in the hills to the right. This is a popular area with cavers who find an intriguing mixture of natural pot holes connecting into old mine workings to explore. Entrance to this underground world may be nothing more romantic than an iron hatch covering a deep shaft. At the gate **3** where the way divides, carry straight on along the bridleway signposted Stockdale Way This is a broad green track through rolling hills with immense views on all sides. It takes you over the watershed and down into the valley of Ribblesdale. No doubt now about the route, as the track winds down the cleft, still with a limestone-splashed hill to one side and a smoother, rounded gritstone slope to the other, with the valley opening out, broad and flat, down below.

On reaching Stockdale Farm, join the surfaced farm approach road which forms the most direct route for continuing on the way, but the wild, craggy scenery over to the right is much too appealing to ignore. So, where the road swings left **4** go through the gate on the right for the footpath towards Settle. Follow the path, with the wall to your left, up to the slope at the foot of Attermire Scar **B** riddled with caves where men lived in the Ice Age over 10,000 years ago. Just before reaching the obvious ladder stile, turn left over a stone stile **5** to take the grassy track heading over the hump. The track narrows down between two stone walls to reach a gate and then winds round the back of the rocky knoll. It is named on the map as Sugar Loaf Hill and you wonder why until you get past it and look back, when it appears as a symmetrical cone which is indeed very like the old-fashioned sugar loaf. That little excursion to the crags over, you reach the farm lane again where you turn right and follow it down to the road **6** where you turn left.

You are now on the minor country road from Settle to Malham, that winds its way through very open countryside. After half a kilometre you reach a patch of woodland and a bridge. Just before crossing the bridge, turn off the road to the right onto the path through the trees that brings you out to the edge of a deep gill, where the falls of Scaleber Force **C** drop sheer from the rock ledge to the stream wandering through the woods. Return to the road and continue on your way, climbing up out of the little valley cut by the stream. Reaching the top of the hill, you can see another stream to the right which has forced a sinuous passage through the land, creating serpentine lines in the folded hills. Now a wide vista opens out to the south of the flatter land beyond the Dales.

Cross the cattle grid, and immediately turn right to a stile **7**.

The approach to Kirkby Malham, a view dominated by the tower of the church known as 'The Cathedral of The Dales'.

Once across continue with the wall on your left over the next two fields of rough, reedy pasture. Just before reaching a ladder stile at a track junction **8**, with a gate on the left, turn left onto the path signposted to Scosthrop Lane and head across the field towards the farm. You will find a ladder stile to the left of the farm which you cross to join the track heading round the back of the little patch of woodland that gives shelter to the house. From here you join the farm approach road that heads out across country and on past the next farm, enjoying extensive views all the way. It is all pleasant, easy walking across fields with a backdrop of rough hills. Cross straight over the road to a stile by the gate and the footpath to Kirkby Malham. The path heads up the slope past old shallow quarries to a gate at the end of the line of trees. Once through the trees, Malham Cove again comes into view, closely followed by Gordale Scar. Head diagonally across the field to the next clump of trees and a gated stile that leads on to a little footbridge. Again trees provide the landmark, as you head off towards the prominent group on the skyline. Cross the stile at the edge of the wood and follow along the side of it towards the village. Now the church provides the marker to direct you to a stile, beyond which stone steps lead on to a stream crossing, after which you arrive at the road and Kirkby Malham church.

The church is remarkably imposing for such a small village, and is popularly known as the Cathedral of the Dales. Due to one of those strange historical quirks whereby kings handed out gifts regardless of geography, this was given to Dereham Abbey in Norfolk by King John in 1199. The canons rebuilt it in 1490 and it was heavily restored in the nineteenth century. The Victorian work is more sensitive than is so often the case, and enough of the old remains to make it worth a visit. Look out, for example, for the sanctuary ring in the very old door which was just what its name suggests – if you grasped hold of that you were assured the protection of the church. Other features include the curious carved niches in the aisle columns, which once held holy figures until they were banished at the Reformation and the box pews, many with their owners' initials and dates, that have been in the church for four centuries.

On leaving the church make your way down to the centre of the village by the pub and turn left at the road junction 9. It is a delightful spot, full of old houses that have sat here solid and durable for three hundred years – even the phone box is venerable, grandly emblazoned with a gold crest. Follow the road round to the right towards Malham. Leaving the village, passing the last of the houses, turn right onto the track by the barn with a tiny, easily missed, footpath sign 10. You immediately turn left onto a path which runs along the edge of the field beside the road, before heading off slightly right towards a stile, with Gordale Scar as a convenient, if distant, marker. The path heads down towards the river bank and a former cotton mill **D**, now converted into holiday homes. Take the path to the left of the buildings which emerges to run beside the old mill leat, which brought water to turn the wheels of industry. Mallard paddle lazily over the calm waters and you reach the mill pond, now largely silted and reedy, but a good habitat for wildfowl. You can still see the weir and sluice gates that controlled the flow of water. The walk continues across the fields by the river, home to oyster catchers and dippers, back to Malham with the limestone face of the Cove as a dramatic backdrop.

Horton in Ribblesdale

The village seems almost overwhelmed by the hills, with limestone escarpments and the deeper man-made scars of quarrying, dominating the slopes to the west and the massive bulk of Pen-y-ghent rising to the east. At its heart it is still an old Dales village of stone houses, clustered round the twin nuclei of church and inn. As a centre it has another great advantage of being a stop on the famously scenic Settle and Carlisle Railway, and indeed the first walk starts from the station itself.

WALK 1 — Ingleborough and Gaping Gill

12.5 miles (20km) See map on pages 36 and 37

The highest of the Three Peaks at 2375 feet (724 metres) Ingleborough is, when approached from Horton, the easiest to climb. Add to the magnificent hill a visit to one of the most famous potholes, a scramble down a limestone gorge and splendid views throughout and you have one of the great Dales walks.

Turn off the main road up to the station **1** and cross over the line at the end of the platform to go up the wooden steps on the far side to join the footpath. Now you get a close view of the gaunt rock face of Horton quarry and the startlingly blue artificial lake at its foot **A**. Turn half right to pass the farm on a clear, well-defined footpath. Where stone has broken through the surface in irregular outcrops, the grassy path gives way to a stonier one bearing away to the right. Turn left by a cairn, and the path is waymarked by yellow topped posts. It is easy to follow in any case as generations of walkers have polished the rock with their boots so that it gleams out from the duller, grey stone. Looking back, there is a fine view over Horton to the distinctive, and rather menacing, dark, brooding bulk of Pen-y-ghent. Reaching a track junction on a grassy plateau, surrounded by fragmented limestone pavement **2** continue straight on along the Ingleborough path towards a cairn on the skyline.

The path heads through a rocky maze of stone blocks and little crags, threaded by long stone walls snaking away up the hillside. The path goes away on a steady, straightforward climb and topping the rise you see the distinctive flat-topped hill of Ingleborough in front of you at the far side of a wide expanse of moor. The well-used path is dotted with cairns, and all the time the underlying stone keeps asserting its presence, breaking out through the peaty surface. The path widens and reaches a track crossing where you still carry on towards the hill already an imposing presence though it is still 3 miles (5km) away. There is another area of rock, worn by wind, rain and frost into sculptural shapes, reminiscent of the works of Henry Moore and Barbara Hepworth – though that should probably be the other way round, as both sculptors were natives of Yorkshire and had known this landscape since childhood. Crossing a ladder stile you see an even more fantastic array of split blocks with boulders perched on top, abandoned thousands of years ago by the retreating ice field. There is a steady climb alongside a tumbling stream, and Ingleborough is temporarily lost from view behind the intervening ridge. Crossing the stream just before the little falls, follow the line of the wall to an old shooting hut, a reminder that we are very much out among the grouse moors. The path rounds the shoulder of the hill where the stream cuts deep into the peat, revealed as a thick black oozy blanket covering the bedrock.

The track leads across the moor again, and now it can be seen running right up to the Ingleborough summit, on a reassuringly gentle slope. It steepens at the end to a path of stone blocks, threading the boulders that surround the plateau to reach the summit **B**. There is time now to take in the wonderfully varied scenery of the Dales, from the natural patterns of limestone pavements and escarpments to the jigsaw-like fields in the valley below. The route now continues along the summit ridge, with a steep drop on the left and on down the saddle separating the main peak from Little Ingleborough. It is like a division between two worlds: to the west out over the flat, rich lands to the sea, to the east the craggy hills.

Reaching the summit of Little Ingleborough **3** with its crazy paving of loose rock slabs, you take the obvious path to the left, winding down into the valley. It begins with a clatter over the stones to a little rock staircase after which a broad, steep path sends you hurrying effortlessly to the valley floor. Where the path divides **4** go to the left to reach Gaping Gill **C**, a genuinely gaping hole in the ground, down which Fell Beck tumbles to reappear after an underground meander at the mouth of Ingleborough Cave. After that little diversion, rejoin the main track and carry on to a ladder stile where you turn right beside the wall to follow the path down

The deep chasm of Trow Gill.

a little stony valley – the beck's original course before it discovered its underground short cut. The path narrows down, plunging steeply through the rocks to a lowering crag, then dives down again between high rock faces for a final scramble to complete the exciting passage of Trow Gill **D**.

The valley now broadens out, with trees to either side of the path, and limestone tamed to minor eruptions. Eventually you arrive at a bridge across the beck that we last met when it was disappearing down Gaping Gill. This time it emerges from Ingleborough Cave **E** where you can pay to take a conducted tour of the floodlit caverns. The track now continues beside the stream. Follow it down almost as far as the woods, then turn left over the footbridge **5** and go straight up the hill to reach the long lane running between stone walls where you turn right. This is an altogether gentler landscape of soft rolling hills with no hard-edged escarpments to interrupt the smooth rise and fall. The walk stays just above the mixed woodland until it reaches a track junction at the end **6** where it turns left on the bridleway to Austwick.

Now, once again the walk is heading back towards the hills, retreating line after line into the far distance, though over to the right you look out over the boundary of the National Park to a different world of fields and woods. The path goes down a dip and you need to look out for a ladder stile on the left **7** which leads to the footpath to Norber. This appears as a broad, green track heading across in front of the crags. Take the rather squelchy path to the corner of the wall below the rock face and follow the wall round to the right to a ladder stile. This stretch of country seems as wild and remote as anything met along the walk as you follow the wall along the foot of the scree spilling down the hillside. A signpost on the skyline points you on your way, still walking in the same direction, now signed to Crummack and heading down between boulders to the wall in front of a clump of trees. Carry on to the little hillock, with the wall to your right, and climb the natural rock staircase. Cross the stile immediately at the top on the right and head across the field to the stile just below the rock outcrop and follow the path round below the crags. Continue down with the wall on your left to the road **8** where you turn left.

The road soon deteriorates to a rough track which climbs gently to a junction **9** where you cross the ladder stile to continue on the path towards Horton. A series of stiles now leads across the fields, the last visible one being in the corner of a field from which you head up beside the wall to a rocky knoll. From here, with more stiles to cross en route, you begin to make your way up to the head of this quiet, remote valley and topping a rise you can see a footbridge across the stream. Once across, turn left to yet another ladder stile **10** which brings you to a green lane where you turn left. Now you head straight into the round scoop at the head of the valley. The lane ends at a gate and the way ahead continues as a clear path through the bracken to reach a plateau and a wide expanse of limestone pavement. You can see a path threading through the stone on the right, heading for a stile in the wall, with a cairn as a useful marker. Now you are heading across the stony upland with Pen-y-ghent rising sternly in front of you. The track follows a line of grouse butts, and once over the stile **11** you turn left along the wall, still crossing a natural pavement, but now a good deal more fragmented. At the next ladder stile, turn away from the wall onto the dark green track that stands out in sharp contrast to the pallid moorland grasses. It runs along the line of a low escarpment to reach a signpost, which should look familiar, for you are back at point **2** which you passed on the way up to Ingleborough. Turn right and retrace your route back to the start.

Cavers preparing for a descent of Gaping Gill. The path winding down from Ingleborough

een in the background.

WALK 2 Pen-y-ghent and the Ribble Valley

10.5 miles (17 km) See map on pages 44 and 45

Walk 1 having taken you up one of the Three Peaks, here is the chance to add a second. The experience, however, is very different and although the hill is lower, it offers a greater challenge. Part of the walk lies over boggy, peat moorland, but the reward for overcoming the difficulties lies with some of the wildest, loneliest scenery in the Dales.

The walk starts near Horton post office on the main road **1** as a rough, stony track running between stone walls and heading very obviously towards the hill. This section forms part of the Pennine Way and Pen-y-ghent itself is a permanent, looming presence just over to the right. There is a good, long, steady slog up the rough track and all the time the scenery is getting wilder, the grass coarser and more and more stone pokes up through the thin cover. This is very uncompromising country – sternly grand rather than conventionally pretty. Over to the right, a gill ends at a crumbling rock face, a giant-sized bite out of the land down which a stream tumbles in a high fall. Just beyond this point **2** the Pennine Way turns off to the right on the obvious path that leads straight up the steep side of Pen-y-ghent then swings round to reach the summit. Anyone wanting a shorter walk could turn off here and resume the description at point **C**. It would be a great shame, however, to miss a truly remarkable sight that lies just a little way ahead.

The main walk goes straight on, leaving the stony path for a grassy path heading off across Horton Moor, an area of coarse grass dotted with treacly brown, impenetrably peaty pools. This brings you to Hull Pot **A**. Here a number of hill streams have united to form a considerable beck which suddenly plunges down into a rocky chasm of overhanging cliffs in a sheer fall to clatter down onto the stony floor where it simply sinks away and disappears from view. From here you turn to the right to cross a ladder stile to continue on the obvious stony path near a little stream which dashes along over falls before doing its own disappearing act and vanishing underground. Reaching a stone wall, you follow it round to the left and on round the corner, so that you are now carrying on in the same direction with the wall on your right. Now you are very much in the middle of the peat moor, with Pen-y-ghent looming up on one side and a swell of low hills on the other. In between lies an expanse of reedy grass and moss and man's presence is limited to a sparse straggle of stone walls. Little streams trickle down from the hills and the walk passes through an area of shake holes, those curious deep hollows that indicate a movement of the rocks somewhere deep below the surface.

Passing through a metal gate, there is a definite change in the landscape as more and more rock begins to break through the surface, and it is time to start looking out for the next turn. It comes just before a wooden gate and is signposted as a footpath heading up the hillside on the right **3**. You head slightly away from the wall and you can see the path twisting up the steep hillside. It goes on getting ever steeper until there is a final scramble up the rocks of the low escarpment. Once over them, a grassy path runs away at an angle from the wall to reach the actual summit of Plover Hill **B**. A stone wall runs right across the top of the hill, crossed by a ladder

The path above Horton on the approach to Pen-y-ghent, part of the Pennine Way.

The view back towards the impressive bulk of Pen-y-ghent, as seen from Helwith Bridge.

stile and once over that you set off to follow the line of the summit ridge, with the rounded hump of Pen-y-ghent ahead of you. After crossing a second stile the whole of the next part of the walk can be clearly seen and there are magnificent views down over Ribblesdale to Ingleborough and beyond that, the third of the peaks, Whernside. The walking along the ridge is like that in the valley over often boggy peat, but any problems that have to be overcome are more than compensated for by the magnificence of the scenery.

A double ladder stile announces the arrival of the summit **C** and here the walk is reunited with the Pennine Way. Once across the stile a very broad stony track is joined that heads off down the hill, with a new and equally appealing perspective of the valley. As on the way up, there is an easy scramble over the rocks of the escarpment, before a very steep, stony path is joined. The path follows the line of the wall on the right, with contrasting views to either side. To the right is the dale, its sides scarred with quarrying, while to the left a solitary, lonely farm peers out over the wastes of the moor. The path once again heads off for the peat, but here the worst sections can be crossed with ease on duckboards which lead to a firm, stony path.

At the track junction **4** by the large pothole Churn Milk Hole, turn right onto the path to Helwith Bridge. The broad track goes through a gate then turns downhill, heading towards the quarry face on the far side of the valley. This soon becomes a very pleasant grassy path that heads through a gradually changing landscape. At first it is surrounded by stone outcrops, with the land divided into big fields of rough grassland. Then as it descends and begins to flatten out, the grass becomes softer, the fields smaller and the first of the trees begin to appear. Instead of just one isolated farm facing a huge expanse of moor, farms now appear at ever shorter intervals, reflecting the increasing richness of the land. Reaching the valley floor **5** turn right onto the track that leads down to the main road. Cross straight over to the minor road opposite which runs across the line of the Settle and Carlisle Railway. Once past the hotel **6** turn right over a ladder stile for the path back to Horton.

Cross over the field to a stile in the far corner to join the quarry road and turn right. Over to the right, the railway crosses the river on a low viaduct, while to the left an isolated terrace of cottages stands high on the hill, built for workers in the adjoining quarry. Where the road turns left, carry straight on under the railway bridge to take the path down to the Ribble. Do not cross the footbridge, but stay on this side of the strongly flowing peaty waters. Where the river sweeps away on a wide bend the route continues down a lane which is unusual for this area, being coolly green and tree-shaded. It ends at a ladder stile and the route continues straight forward past the prominent tree in the centre of the field to rejoin the river bank. Near the end of this section, there is a pleasant interlude where the path wanders up into a little copse. Then, where a road appears alongside on the left, look out for a footbridge on the right that takes you across a little stream and back down to the river again. For most of the way, the river has been strong and steady, but it has a final roar as it swings round a sharp bend at the edge of Horton. Stay with the riverside walk until you reach two bridges, a stone road bridge and the wooden footbridge which you cross to arrive at the car park next to the main road in Horton.

Ingleton

A dramatic village, where two rivers, the Twiss and the Doe, roar through and unite to form the Greta. Over them all looms the tall viaduct that once carried the railway from Clapham to Sedbergh. With both Ingleborough and Whernside close at hand, this is an understandably popular walking centre.

WALK 1 — Whernside and Ribblehead
14.5 miles (23 km) or 12 miles (19km) See map on pages 50 – 53

This walk includes the ascent of the third of the Three Peaks, crosses a splendid limestone pavement and ends along a Roman road.

There are two basic options for this walk. The longer involves walking out of Ingleton, completing the circuit and returning again. The second is to drive to a point on the circuit – Chapel-le-Dale for example would be appropriate – and reduce the distance by 2.5 miles (4 km). The description is given for the full walk. Even here there is a choice for instead of using the road, as described, the Waterfalls Walk, up or down the Doe, could be included. Part of the Waterfalls Walk is included in Walk 2, where there is a full description. It sounds a bit complicated, but all should soon be clear.

From the centre of Ingleton, cross the bridge over the Doe **1** and immediately turn right onto the minor road climbing up the hill, with the wooded river valleys to either side. Coming out into the open, the route passes old quarries. Where the road turns sharp right **2**, turn left up the little lane to Twisleton Scar End. At the track junction by the farm **3** turn left onto the wide, stony track, and you are now on the circular walk. About 100 yards after going through the gate, just before the track begins to level out and makes a slight turn to the right, turn right onto the grassy path, a definite indentation curling up the shoulder of the hill. It climbs up to the little limestone outcrop, then doubles back on itself and now you can look down the Twiss valley to the Ingleton viaduct and listen to the roar from Thornton Force.

The track soon reaches an area where stone predominates, and here the track swings round to the left and climbs up to a limestone pavement. Head straight forward for the edge of the scar on the

Looking across the fractured limestone pavement of Twistleton Scar to the distinctive, stepped shape of Ingleborough.

skyline to reach a very obvious green track that swings away to the left through scattered stone blocks. A rough path leads up to the cairn on Ewes Top, and one of the most remarkable of all the natural pavements of the region. It looks as if a giant has attacked the rock with a hammer, splitting it in all directions which, in a sense, is just what has happened, though the giant is the weather and his tools the wind, rain and frost. Whernside looms up like a stranded whale: you are at the tail and the head still lies some miles away. The walk continues through the very fractured landscape of weathered stone, through which a little stony path threads its way. Then, passing a large isolated boulder, head off across a more open section of moor and, passing the edge of the pavement, a new path has been waymarked, which should be kept to, as it has been rerouted to avoid erosion. Everywhere there are shake holes and pot holes, the tops of which have often been weathered into strange shapes – one in particular has been given a fluted rim, like an Elizabethan ruff. To add to the enjoyment, the walking itself is easy on a well-defined path. Along the way are a number of erratics, boulders balanced on spindly plinths above the pavement. Where grass has grown over the stone it has produced a curious humpy landscape, as though hundreds of super-energetic moles have been at work.

Reaching a path junction **4** turn left and now stretches of peaty moor appear among the stone and you look up the valley to the tall striding arches of Ribblehead viaduct. There are more changes ahead as patches of woodland appear and you head off towards the farm set among trees. This brings you to a ford which you cross to join the farm path. Pass in front of the farm **A** to take the wide track that winds round the hill, on the slope of which trees contrive to grow through a wilderness of boulders. Pass another farm, much changed over the years – the oldest part has the date 1689 over the door. Just beyond that where the track divides **5** carry straight on, then turn immediately left where the path can be all too clearly seen heading up the very steep hillside to Whernside summit. It proves to be not only a demanding but a frustrating climb. Reaching what appears to be the top **6** you turn right and climb again to another top, and then yet another until the trig point **B** finally confirms that the climb really is over. How splendid it is though, with both Ingleborough and Pen-y-ghent in view, the line of the Settle and Carlisle railway snaking away below you, crossing the Ribblehead and Dent Head viaducts and in the far distance the Howgill Fells and Lakeland mountains.

Continue straight on along the path to begin the descent to a peaty moor and dotted with pools and meres. The early part of the way is built up of stone blocks, keeping you clear of the mire, but once across the stream this reverts to a conventional path. At the track junction **7** turn right towards Ribblehead. On the hillside opposite you can see a line of air shafts from the railway tunnel, with the spoil excavated during construction piled all around them. You reach the valley floor beside a dashing stream, dropping down the gill in a series of falls. Cross over the railway. Over to the left is the tunnel entrance, and over to the right an aqueduct with a stepped-stone lining to carry the hill stream on its way, eventually to join the River Doe. The track follows the line of the railway until it reaches a dilapidated signalman's cottage and the signal box **8**. Turn right to go under the railway bridge, cross the beck by the farm and join the surfaced farm road. At the junction **9** turn left and follow the farm road down to an actual minor road which bridges the beck – or would do if the beck had not temporarily ducked out of sight, leaving a dry, stony bed. At a cattle grid **10** leave the road for the path on the right which heads for the gate at the angle between two walls. Cross the field with the wall on your left to reach the brook which has reappeared only to promptly vanish again. Go through the gate to follow the stream bed – you can actually hear it tumbling along just below the surface. At the next gate follow the line of the wall on the left to join a very overgrown, sunken path. This emerges at a surfaced road where you turn left **11** and it brings you out on the main road near the inn. Turn right past the old school, now a bunkhouse, and at the next road junction turn right into Chapel-le-Dale.

The road passes the tiny church **C**, as simple inside as out, with a memorial to the men who lost their lives building the Settle and Carlisle Railway. The road bends round to the village houses and all route finding problems disappear for a while, for you are now following the course of a Roman road, which if not exactly ruler straight is near enough. It stays with the Doe valley floor, with Ingleborough on one side and Whernside on the other. It is very quiet and there are wide grassy margins. It is a pleasant walk and always full of interest, whether it is an old quarry with a waterfall coursing down its face or a rather grim farmhouse, which seems to belong in a Brontë novel. The famous White Scar caves can be seen up on the road to the left. Reaching the top of the Waterfalls Walk **12** turn right on the footpath to Scar End, an obvious path running up the hillside, with a working quarry to the left, which brings you out by Scar End Farm **3** where you turn left to return to the start.

This begins with a dramatic waterfall walk, visits one of the lonelier valleys and ends with a gentler stroll through farmland and the attractive Greta valley. There is even a brief excursion into Lancashire!

This walk like the first starts at the centre, crosses the Doe, but then goes on to cross the Twiss **1**. Here you turn right to join the Waterfalls Walk. The Walk was developed following the arrival of the railway which opened Ingleton up for tourism. An Improvement Association was formed and the walks along the Doe and the Twiss created in 1885. There is a modest charge – less than you pay for some Dales car parks – and it is worth every penny. While not, in general, favouring charges for enjoying what is, after all, a natural phenomenon, this is just too good to miss. The walk only includes the Twiss, but the Doe could be incorporated into the previous Whernside walk.

How spectacular the walk turns out to be depends very much on the weather, and it is certainly at its best after heavy rain, as it was when this description was written. From the very start, the river roars along through the narrows, with high cliffs rising above the water. It looks like cappuccino fired through a water cannon, a huge brown river with a foaming, frothy, creamy head. The path itself is very natural, rising and falling below the cliffs, crossing and recrossing the river. It seems suitably grand until you reach the Pecca Falls **A** which surpass anything seen so far. The water thunders over a ledge, and this you soon find is just the first of a series of falls all contained within a tight, twisting rocky gully against the sides of which the water beats and sends the spray flying. After that the path emerges onto moorland, with the river rushing down below in its ravine. The excitement seems to be over, but the highest falls are saved for last. The river drops over a series of ledges, then tipples over the lip to create Thornton Force **B** plunging into the pool far below. The path climbs up beside the falls and follows the river to Ravenray Bridge. Cross over and climb the hillside opposite to reach a broad green track **2** where you turn left.

Now you are out on the moor with limestone escarpments rising above scree-spattered slopes. The track crosses the river, now considerably tamed, and officially reduced in status to a beck wandering down the narrow Kingsdale valley. Continue on to the road where you turn left and after about 50 yards, turn right over a ladder stile **3**. The route heads straight uphill to another stile silhouetted on the skyline. It is at any rate straight on the map, but in practice you have to find the best route you can up through the confusion of blocks that make up the escarpment. Reaching the stile, you can look back over the lower slopes of Whernside to Ingleborough. Once again, the route goes up through a stony jumble to reach a small plateau and over to the left you can see a massive, precariously perched boulder known as the Cheese Press Stone **C**. The simplest way to continue is to turn right along the wide, flat ledge towards the long wall rising up the hillside: keep more or less parallel to this wall and you will not go astray as you climb up to a series of platforms, each rising a little lower than the last. Eventually the way ahead is crossed by a wall. Go through the gate and continue on to the wide track **4** where you turn left.

Now you are high up on the wild moor at the edge of the National Park. There is an immense view in front of you, all the way

The dramatic falls of Thornton Force.

to Morecambe Bay, overlooked by a massive square building which might look like some medieval fortress but is actually Heysham power station. The track heads steadily downhill between stone walls, then runs straight on as a surfaced road. The fields begin to lose their rusty tinge and develop a richer, lusher green, while the road bends and twists through a hummocky landscape, eventually reaching the valley floor by a grand old stone house, cosily wrapped in sheltering trees. You pass a footpath on the left to Masongill Hall and immediately beyond that, where the road swings sharp left **5** turn right through the gate to take the path beside the wall. Beyond the next gate, the path swings left round the hillock to join a little lane that briefly runs between stone walls to emerge above the beck. Follow the line of the wall on the left and you come out above romantic, castellated Over Hall. From the gate make your way down to the obvious track running from the hall to the village of Ireby and you are now in Lancashire.

This is a most attractive spot with little greens and a stream bustling through the middle. Follow the main street down by the stream to the road junction, where you turn left. Where the houses end **6** turn right onto the surfaced path leading up to an isolated house. Go past it to a gate and take the path across the field to the road. Cross straight over to take the farm road opposite which goes between what are obviously bridge parapets **D** – but there is no bridge, and nothing to be crossed. Look to the left, however, and you can see what is clearly a railway bridge, so you are walking across the filled in cutting on the disused line from Ingleton.

Reaching the farm, turn left by the first of the old barns **7** then right to go round the farmhouse at an angle from the wall to reach a stile in a stone wall. Cross the field to a footbridge, then turn right to join the farm track that swings round to the left. There is now a much clearer path to follow across the fields with the stone wall to the left. There is a very open prospect and it is noticeable that here, on the fringes of the Dales, the land is a good deal richer. Pass a little hummock with a wall to your right and continue on to the stile where you can see your next objective, the spire of Burton in Lonsdale church rising up in front of you. Passing the farm, join the lane briefly, continuing in the same direction, then go through the next gate to return to walking across the fields, swinging off to the left to cross the stream. This is *not* at the obvious ford used by cattle. Go a little way to the left of that and step across the stream to reach a stile. Continue with the fence on your right and head off to a point between the old farmhouse and the more modern house to reach the next stile. Now the way continues via gates and stiles (one of the stiles needs searching out as it is tucked away in the corner of the field) heading towards the prominent clump of trees. Soon you get a clear view of the church with a large mound beside it **E**. Getting nearer, you can also make out earthworks in front of it. This is all that remains of a Norman motte and bailey: the keep sat on the motte or mound, with the defended courtyard, the bailey, in front. Head off to the road to the left of the church which you go straight up to reach the main road **8** where you turn left.

At the road junction, follow the main road round to the left, and you immediately come to a footpath sign on the right **9** which appears to point up the drive of a private house. In fact, it immediately turns off to the right as a narrow lane running between the houses. This brings you down to a footbridge over a stream tumbling down a weir. Coming up out of the little valley, continue in the same direction between the barns, with the straggling remains of a hedge, now reduced to a few thorn bushes on your left. An old gatepost on the skyline provides a useful marker that leads you on to a ladder stile, now with the great hunched shoulder of Ingleborough ahead of you. Continue over the fields via stiles – one, crossing a newly planted hedge, is a sort of mini-footbridge – and end up at a stile beside the gate leading to the road **10**.

Turn right then left over the stile at the foot of the hill to follow the line of the fence on the right. At the next gate, turn half right for a pair of stiles in the far corner to follow the path still heading towards Ingleborough. Topping the rise, the final objective comes into view as you look down onto Ingleton, and now you can see the next stile. Head past the farmhouse, and go through the gate that leads to a path down towards the river bend, following the fence on the left. As the river starts to swing away look for a stile rather hidden away among the trees, not far below the level of the fence. This takes you into a wood under an archway of gnarled and twisted branches. You now get quite close to the Greta as it swirls vigorously round a bend. You emerge into a little glade, where a footbridge takes you over a tributary stream. Make your way across the fields and now the river begins to swing again and path and water come ever closer until they reunite just before reaching New Bridge **11**. Cross a stile, climb the steps to the road and cross over the bridge. Take the first left turn for the road back into Ingleton, with the viaduct striding over the valley in front of you.

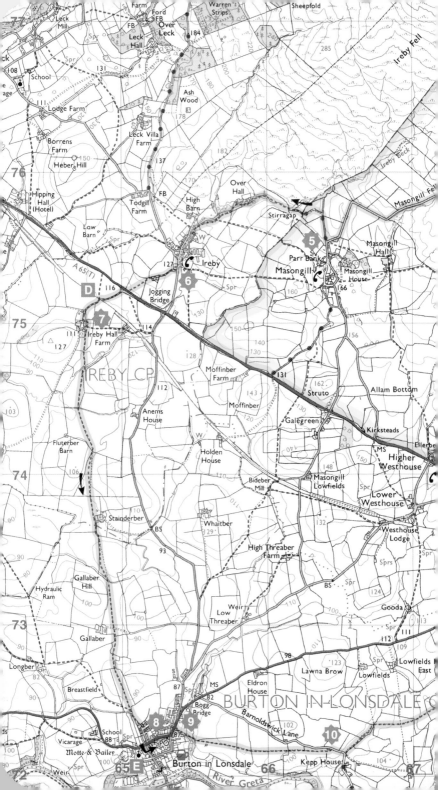

The Cheese Press - a delicate balancing act on the limestone pavement at Keld Head.

Hawes

One of the most popular centres in the Dales, a market town of cobbled streets and little alleys, it has the added attraction of a waterfall in the heart of the town. Other attractions include the creamery where Wensleydale cheese has been made since 1897, a traditional rope maker and a folk museum on the site of the old Wensleydale railway station.

WALK I Appersett and Hardraw

13.5 miles (22km) See map on pages 66 and 67

A walk that provides a splendid mixture: riverside walks in the valleys, magnificent high level walks with superb views, rough open moor and woodland paths.

Leave the town on the A 684 Sedbergh road, and follow it round to the right past the Ingleton turn. Opposite the first farm on the right, turn left onto the farm track signposted as a footpath to Thorney Mire House **1**. At the first gateway, turn half right to a stile in the wall just beyond the trees. Cross a stream and take the second of the two stiles on the right. Continue in the same direction, but now with the wall on the left. After crossing a ladder stile, turn away from the wall to head for the brow of the hill and topping the rise you will see the next objective, an impressive stone viaduct **A**. The railway opened in 1875 and ran the length of Wensleydale to join the Settle and Carlisle at Garsdale – and a splendidly scenic route it must have been for those lucky enough to travel it before its closure in 1959.

On reaching the viaduct, turn right down the road beside Widdale Beck, which races down towards the Ure over a series of flat, stone ledges. This brings you to Appersett where you cross the beck on the stone bridge. Once over, cross the low stile on the left and immediately turn right beside the wall on the path to Mossdale Head. This brings you down to a second bridge, but this time over the Ure **2**, where you turn left to begin an attractive riverside walk. The path is grassy, the river runs clear, faintly tinged with peaty brown, over a stony bed. Mallards paddle along under the shade of the trees, and here and there marsh marigolds spring up at the water's edge to brighten the way. The path wanders up through a patch of woodland, then after crossing a ladder stile the riverside is temporarily deserted. Head off round to the left of the wood, passing a venerable oak which has thrown a massive branch across the path, that bows to the ground and then rises again to create a natural arch. Topping the little hill, the way ahead holds promise of wilder scenery.

Coming down the other side of the hillock to rejoin the river, the sweet hay meadows have been left behind for coarser moorland grasses and the hillside is scarred with old quarry tips. A ladder stile gives access to a path through a wood dominated by a fine mixture of mature beech and oak, before coming right back down to the river bank. Crossing a small stream brings a return of the hay meadows. Turn left towards the gate to the right of the barn and follow the path round, keeping the wall on the right and on leaving the field turn left on the farm road. Where the track divides **3** carry straight on passing the farm on your right to enter a peaceful wooded valley, where even the birdsong seems hushed, apart from the occasional staccato piping of wagtails. After quite a long absence, the path converges on the long line of trees that marks the course of the river, and soon rejoins it. The valley floor is flat, the meadows rich with wild flowers, but looking ahead it is quite clear that all this is about to change, as the hills steepen and low, gleaming escarpments appear at the summits.

Reaching the farm, take the path between the house and the barn to emerge by Mossdale Head viaduct **B**, its arches framing the falls on Mossdale Beck. Carry on through the gate and turn right on the path up the hill. Just before reaching the top, turn right beside the wall to cross a stile and continue on the path through reedy moorland, waymarked by yellow arrows. This brings you down to the main road which you cross straight over to the bridge across the stream and the path climbing up through the trees. Once clear of these, the open hillside rises ahead of you. The path heads straight up the steep slope, aiming for the end of the line of trees where there is a ladder stile. Apart from a natural inclination to pause for breath, it is worth stopping occasionally to enjoy the wide views over Wensleydale. At first there is no obvious path, but once you have crossed a cobbled way a definite landmark appears in the form of conifers on the skyline and you head off towards them. It is a tough climb through tussocky, reedy grass, but it soon presents a more than adequate reward.

On reaching the gate by the trees **4** turn left onto the track beside the plantation, passing an old lime kiln that makes a popular shady retreat for sheep, and here a memorial bench gives you a chance to sit and enjoy the view, and how splendid it is, looking straight down the deep valley of the Cotterdale Beck. The hard work is over for a while and the walk continues along The High Way that follows the wall at the rim of the valley. Now the going is easy on soft turf and the views are superb, looking towards Garsdale Head and the viaduct of the Settle and Carlisle Railway with its background of high fells. There is little to disturb the peace – unless you come on weekdays when you look *down* on RAF jets playing chase up and down the dale. Otherwise the sheep munch, kestrels hover and stonechats natter. Limestone bubbles up through the grass and you can enjoy as good a long stretch of high level walking as you can find in the area.

The final section turns into a rutted track which leads to a turning point by the farm buildings **5**. Here you turn right back at an acute angle onto a very indistinct path across the moor, but there are waymarkers in the form of yellow topped posts. Now the turf gives way to typical moorland of reedy grass, sphagnum moss and speckles of white cotton grass. This is very open landscape with no obvious guiding features apart from the marker posts. You can see grouse butts over to the right, with the high hill of Widdale Fell rising on the far side of the valley. Eventually, when you top the rise, you have a definite landmark to head for. A line of butts stretches along the skyline, looking from a distance rather like a row of sheds. Head towards them, but before you get to them there is a stream to cross. You can see it bends round to the right to cross the line of the walk, and the easiest crossing is to be found a little downstream of the bend. Once over, pass through the line of grouse butts to the corner of the fenced enclosure, and once again the path is quite faint. There is no real problem, however, for once again you cross a rise, and the route becomes clear, following the line of the gully on the right towards the forestry plantation spread in front of you with an obvious break in the trees **6**.

Cross a stile to head down the wide fire break with dense conifers to either side. A word of caution here: this description was accurate when the author did the walk, but forests are constantly changing as some areas are felled and new roads are driven through. The good news is that not much can go wrong providing you keep heading downhill towards the road in the Cotterdale valley. Cross straight over the forest road by the waymarkers and follow the yellow markers down to the road 7. Cross over the road by two small footbridges to reach a stile, then boulder hop across the stream to reach another stile and turn left towards a ladder stile that brings you to a stony road where you turn right.

Leave the road to cross the beck by the footbridge **8** which leads you into Cotterdale Woods where there is a little picnic area, from which a path leads up beside the stream to a rough path that emerges by the forest road. There is now a long, steady climb up through the trees to a major track junction **9** where you turn right. This soon arrives at a second junction where you turn left, still climbing. The path doubles back on itself for the final climb out of the woods. You have now arrived at Abbotside Common, where you turn right onto the bridleway **10** and, you may note with some relief, a level track. Now you are back with easy walking on grassland amid scampering rabbits, with wide vistas over dale and fells. And as you pass the end of the woodland, so the views get even better. Soon you join the Pennine Way, coming down over the hill on the left, after which you cross a ladder stile to begin the descent to Hawes, now visible in the valley.

The grassy track gives way to an altogether rougher track that seems to get steeper and steeper as it drops down to the road at Hardraw **11**. Turn left across the bridge. If you are still feeling energetic you can, for a modest fee, stop off here for a visit to Hardraw Force **C,** which falls from an overhanging rock face, dropping 90 feet (27 metres). Once over the bridge, turn right over the stile, still on the Pennine Way, for a little paved path across the fields. The walk brings you down to the convoluted River Ure and passes a sweeping bend to head for the road **12**. Turn right along the road to cross the low, double-arched road bridge. Where the road turns left, carry straight on along the footpath, cutting off a large bend in the road, before rejoining it for the walk back into Hawes.

The view from The High Road, looking across to Garsdale Head viaduct.

WALK 2 Semer Water and Bainbridge

12.5 miles (20km) See map on pages 74 and 75

This walk visits two beautiful watercourses, and a lake. In between are walks over the hills and down a Roman road.

The walk starts by leaving the main street under an archway between the shops and is signposted, just inside the arch, as the Pennine Way **1**. It leads down a ginnel or alley alongside the church-yard. A squeeze stile leads out to the fields and a flagstone path leading towards Gayle with its background of high fells. Head off across the shoulder of the hill with the beck to your left. Up ahead, on the outskirts of the village, is a substantial water mill, which surprisingly in this country of sheep and wool, was built in the eighteenth century to spin cotton **A**. Turn left at the road. Do not continue on the Pennine Way, but carry on up the road to the centre of the village. Turn left over the bridge under which the beck cascades in a series of low falls over rock ledges. This little beck changes very dramatically with the weather, and you may find anything from a gentle trickle to a peaty, frothing torrent. Follow the road round away from the beck as it begins to climb up the hill and at the end of the first field on the left, turn up the stone steps to the stile and the footpath to Yorburgh **2**.

Start by following the wall to the left, then head off right towards the barn by the prominent tree to find a stile in the wall. Carry on to the next stile and turn right through the little gate by the farm gate and immediately left onto the path running between stone walls. Each of the fields comes complete with its own barn and you pass the farm itself over to the left. Reaching the little wood where ash trees hang their branches over the way, keep with the lane as it turns sharply to the left. Go through a gate and a tumbled down stone wall, and now the path heads at an angle from the wall, recognisable as a slight indentation heading up the hill. This is now a pleasant grassy path, running beside small quarries. You reach a gate on the left and carry on to the next gate, still following the contours of the hill towards a signpost on the skyline **3**. Here you turn right to head more steeply uphill. Cross a stone stile and carry on with the stream to your left at first. Cross the stream just above the little waterfall and carry on uphill with no obvious marker for a while. Eventually you will see the corner of a wall on the hill above you. Head to the left of that and if you then look up to the wall above you, you will see a prominent yellow paint blob marking the stile **4**.

Once over the stile, turn right to follow the line of the wall and continue in the same direction on the obvious grassy path heading through the rough moor, where the plaintive cry of the curlew competes with the cheerful tune of the pipit. A rutted track is followed through a gap in the wall and then swings right as a stony path winding its way up to the top of Wether Fell, with a splendid panorama of hills all around you. Where the rutted track turns away to the right **5** carry straight on along the grass path, heading up towards a much more prominent track, which is converging from the left. At this track **6** turn left and you have now joined the Roman Cam High Road. It does not do what Roman roads are supposed to do, for it goes almost at once round a sharp bend, and after that it runs on in a slight curve before finally achieving a satisfactory Roman straightness. The old track is worn right down to the bedrock, not surprising perhaps after nearly 2000 years of use.

After the road has straightened, turn right through a gate to join the bridleway of Crag Side Road **7**. Now you look down on lovely

Looking back down the paved footpath to Hawes church at the start of the walk towards Gayle.

remote and wild Raydale, a narrow valley, closed in by softly rounded hills. Where the way divides, stay with the bridleway which changes from a rutted track to a more pleasant broad, green track through the coarse grass, from which the occasional grouse erupts with a manic flurry of wings. The view ahead is now dominated by the hill of Addlebrough with its prominent escarpment. On reaching a little line of crags where the way divides **8** turn right onto the footpath. Go through the wall by the footpath sign to reach the brow of the hill and now the path appears as a faint green line heading down to the valley floor and the village of Marsett, with Semer Water gleaming away to the left. There is a steep descent over a series of stiles and now the familiar curlew are joined by black headed gulls flying up from the lake. The path leads to a farm track where you turn left to reach the road by Marsett Bridge **9**.

Turning left at the road you get a typical Dales contrast of rich pasture on the valley floor, ending very abruptly at the lower slopes of the moor. At the end of the last Ice Age all this area was covered by the meltwater of the glacier, held back by a natural dam. It silted up creating the rich land through which you are walking and Semer Water is now all that is left of a lake that was 3 miles (5 km) long. This quiet road is followed past traditional Carr End farm, with a less traditional caravan park alongside it, followed by the imposing entrance to Wood End Lodge. The road dips and climbs again as it crosses a small stream, then after levelling out, heads downhill again. Before reaching the foot of the hill **10** turn right onto the footpath for Semer Water Bridge. The path heads down through the trees and follows the edge of the field, continuing with the wall on the left to reach a reedy area with yellow waymarkers. It wanders into a little copse to emerge by the handsome stone bridge **B** at the end of the lake. This is not an entirely peaceful spot at weekends, as it used for water skiing, but that does nothing to detract from the natural beauty.

Once over the bridge, turn left onto the riverside path. At first the river is very placid, meandering between reedy banks and where it goes through one of its wide, sweeping bends, the still waters of the shallows have allowed colourful displays of water lily to develop. After the walk over the hills, this is a contrasting stroll through meadows among gently rising hills. But then, after a footbridge across a reedy tributary, the river swings away and the path goes straight on over a ladder stile to climb Bracken Hill. It is certainly not the highest hill in the area, but it does provide a grand panorama. Over to the left the River Bain has plunged away down a wooded gorge. Looking back, there is Semer Water, more beautiful than ever set in the bowl of the hills, and one looks across to a farm with as good a vantage point for enjoying the scenery as you could wish. Now an obvious path leads back down to the river, now falling over flat, rock ledges, and you stay with it all the way down to the main road **11** where you leave the fields by a squeeze stile that certainly lives up to its name and turn left into Bainbridge.

Cross the bridge to the village centre with its wide green and old inn, and then turn immediately left onto the dead end road, passing the nineteenth century dame school where the three Rs were taught for a fee of two pence per week. Where the road ends, continue with the wall on your right, on the footpath signposted to Semer Water. It looks unlikely as it starts by going through someone's garden, but it is a genuine right of way. The path now follows the opposite bank of the Bain along the rim of the valley, so that you now get a much better view of the river as it rushes down its deep gorge. The path heads across the fields towards the farmhouse on the skyline, crossing a small stream en route. It passes a marker post in the middle of the field to emerge to the right of the farmhouse **12**. Turn right onto the track that leads down to the road, where you turn right and having climbed up out of the valley you now, somewhat perversely, have to head down again for a short way. Where the road swings sharp right **13** turn left onto the long straight track, back once again on the Roman road.

For the next mile or so, there is no need to worry about route finding, so there is ample time to enjoy the views over Wensleydale from this hill top track. It ends at the road **14** where you turn right, and now the long, steady climb ends as you turn back down into the valley. The road goes through a U bend to cross Horton Gill with its procession of falls, after which the road straightens to pass old quarries and a lime kiln. Another stream is crossed, its banks bright with blood-drop emlets, before reaching the village of Burtersett **C.** Once again, the old stone houses get together in a companionable huddle for mutual protection against the harshness of winter. Follow the road down through the village, and immediately past the old converted chapel, turn left through the gap in the houses for the footpath to Hawes. Now, like the path out to Gayle, there is an old inter-village route of flagstones, leading via a procession of stiles across the fields. On crossing the road, turn slightly left to continue on the flagstone path that leads to the main road where you turn left for the centre of Hawes.

Reeth

Where so many villages sit snugly on the valley floors, Reeth enjoys an airy site above the Swale. With its broad green and cobbled market, it was once an important centre for the local lead mining industry, which explains the size and grandeur of the old inns.

WALK 1 | The Swale Valley and Arkengarthdale

12 miles (18km) See map on pages 80 and 81

After a gentle introduction to Swaledale, the walk heads up to the high lonely moors with extensive remains of old mines, and returns down the narrow valley of Arkengarthdale

From the green in the centre **1** take the road down past the eighteenth-century Kings Arms and the Black Bull Hotel with its bizarre, upside-down sign. Reaching the end of the green, turn right to follow the footpath down towards the river. Turn left at the T-junction, then right down the dead end road which passes the playground and then becomes a rough track. From here you look down on the Swale, which is going through a series of elaborate meanders. Where the track comes to an end, continue straight on through the small gate by the farm gate for a clear path across the hay meadows via a series of stiles. You can see a suspension bridge over the river, which is still pursuing its erratic course, wandering up near the path then sliding away again. Gradually the path climbs up towards the road across sandy banks full of rabbit holes, whose inhabitants scamper everywhere. It is all very pleasant, easy walking which ends at the road by the village of Healaugh.

Turn left along the road and then at the road junction **2** turn right up the minor gated road that soon begins to climb and wind steeply uphill to emerge in the open on a hillside of grass and bracken. It ends at the farmhouse **A** with a magnificent view out over Swaledale, and continues forward as a farm track on the left. Where tracks divide just past the farm **3** take the one on the right heading through heather with a line of grouse butts on the skyline up ahead. Passing the sheepfolds this becomes a very attractive moorland path, and where paths again divide **4** keep to the obvious line on the left. This becomes a pleasant grassy track beside the wall

This attractive stream is crossed on the walk through the wild landscape of Reeth Low Moor.

that now begins to turn away down to the valley. It reaches a lovely little spot where a stream bubbles over rocks and curlew and lapwing exchange cries overhead. Take the path down to the ford and continue up the other side by the fence to join the road **5**.

Turn right onto the road which dips down to a footbridge by a ford, then climbs up the hill on the far side. On reaching the brow of the hill **6** turn left onto the bridleway which heads up towards more grouse butts, and certainly the birds are plentiful on these moors. Beyond the butts, the track climbs to an area of old mine shafts and spoil heaps. Now you look down to the right to Arkengarthdale and the village of Langthwaite. Where the track divides **7** keep to the left, heading up towards a very lumpy landscape. You arrive at an area heavily scarred by mining, riven by the deep hushes where miners washed away the surface soil to expose the ore-bearing rocks, and piled high with spoil **B**. No one would call this pretty, but here surrounded by heather moorland there is an eerie austere beauty. The track runs along the edge of the hill, with the spoil heaps to the left. Reaching the end of the line of tips by an area of stony land and a small cairn **8** you double right back onto a grassy path that soon begins to head off down the hillside. It wanders through more old workings before heading down again and there is a splendid view of the dale with its extraordinarily complex pattern of fields of all shapes and sizes spreading up the opposite hillside. This is an enjoyable descent on a comfortable zig-zagging path. Follow the path round behind the last of the pits and spoil heaps to make for the obvious track junction beside the sheepfold on the valley floor **9**. Turn right here down to the road **10** where you turn left, then right at the first junction to head down across Whaw Bridge **11**.

Once across the bridge turn right onto the footpath in front of the barn, and now the rough moorland tracks are exchanged for easy footpaths across the riverside fields. On the left, the hillside is divided into small fields, regularly dotted with field barns, and there is a suggestion of an old cobbled way peeping through the grass. The path runs for a time beside the clear waters of Arkle Beck, then temporarily deserts it for a visit to the woodland. The fields return for a while, but soon the path dives back into the dark, ferny woods, where gnarled old trees spread their roots round mossy boulders. Leave the wood by the gate in the wall and you are back in the fields again alongside the river, now shaded by ash, sycamore and rowan. The way ahead continues by gates and stile towards the road. In the last field before reaching it, turn right to cross a footbridge, created out of a single, massive baulk of timber **12** and once across continue in the same direction on the riverside walk.

Cross straight over the road and continue on the footpath. This arrives at the approach road to sternly imposing Scar House in a wooded setting across the river. Turn left towards the river, then immediately right to cross a stile and follow the grand parade of trees that leads across the fields to Arkengarthdale church **C**. This is Georgian and not as it might appear at first glance Victorian, and inside is a rather surprising panelled ceiling. Continue on down the roadside path into Langthwaite. Turn left to cross the river and turn right opposite the Red Lion. This is a pleasant spot to linger – and not just for the obvious attraction – for the scene is full of charm, with a small stream bustling down to join the beck near the bridge. The path passes the chapel of 1839, built by Methodists whose enthusiasm earned them the name of Ranters. Now we are back with the riverside walk across the fields with extensive views over the dale.

The walk stays on this bank, ignoring the various footbridges, passing along the edge of the wood and finally entering it, and very fine woodland it is too with mature beech competing with tall fir for domination. Where the path divides **13** turn right to go through a short tunnel which takes you under the old transport route from the mines up the hillside. After that industrial interlude the pleasant walk over fields is resumed, with the beck much swollen, running fast and peaty over its stony bed. Crossing a foot-bridge over a stream brings an area of even richer meadows before a wood is reached and an obstacle course of tangled roots. Then, as the river turns away, the footpath, waymarked in yellow, heads straight on across the fields and through the pine trees. Where a stream is crossed, the beck sets off on a big bend, and the path heads away for a house on the skyline below a scree-covered slope. Once over the hill and through a collapsed wall there is a brief reunion at the water's edge and then another woodland diversion. Although you are still more or less following the line of the beck on its way down the valley, the path itself is now higher up the hill, running through a confusion of rocks and bracken. Finally this switchback route ends with a view of Reeth down in the valley.

At the road **14** turn right and then, at the next road junction, turn right again. Where the road goes steeply downhill, turn right onto the path, following the wall on the left, not the more obvious farm track. Now there is a plain path across the fields to the road, where you turn right to cross the bridge to return to the centre of Reeth.

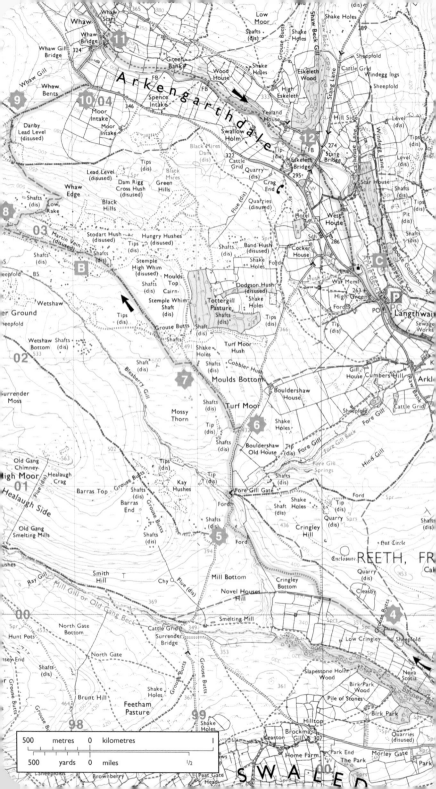

WALK 2 · Muker and Keld

10.5 miles (17km) See map on pages 86 and 87

The walk starts at Gunnerside a little way up the valley from Reeth, but it is well worth making the journey, for this is a walk of high drama and great variety, with deep gorges, waterfalls and high moors.

Start by the bridge in Gunnerside **1**, where there is parking available. Take the road past the village stores and the school to join the footpath to Ivelet. This runs past the houses to emerge as a very obvious path across the fields, with the usual array of stiles to act as markers. Arriving at the river bank do *not* cross the stile, but follow the line of the fence above the river, enjoying this very attractive stretch of the Swale. There is a dip down through a little wood to a footbridge over a stream and you emerge on the other side at the little village of Ivelet. Cross straight over the road to join the footpath to Muker. There is now a pleasant, easy, high level walk across the fields, where rabbits abound and the occasional pheasant wanders out of the wood with that rather vague air that all pheasants seem to have. Reaching the farm buildings **2** cross the yard to the stile by the gate, passing the very handsome house, for the path heading downhill in the direction of Muker. You pass a new plantation of trees, an unusually good variety of broad-leaved species, not the ubiquitous spruce.

The walk comes down from the fields to a riverside path, but it is a short lived union. The river wanders away and the path turns to the right across the fields, following the lower slope of the hill. Where the path divides **3** turn left to take the path down to and across the footbridge. Turn right beside the river then follow the path up to the barn **4**. Double back to take the path heading up the hill to the top corner of the field, where you join a little shady lane. This eventually emerges above Muker **5** onto a zig-zag stony path up the hill with a view out to the road snaking up to Butter Tubs Pass. Before reaching the top of the hill **6** turn right by the old farmhouse to join the Pennine Way. This brings you to a narrow path along the valley rim and as fine a high level walk as you will find in the whole of the Dales. Down below the river is a silvery ribbon through startlingly green fields as it emerges from a deep ravine. The path gets ever rougher as it threads through rocks and craggy outcrops, and you can look across to Swinner Gill and its waterfall which will soon be visited. The path narrows, the hillside steepens and progress slows as you pick your way through the rocks. Where the valley view is lost behind

The walk near Muker, a landscape in which it seems every field comes complete with its own barn.

The desolate ruins of Crackpot Hall, looking down the narrow valley leading into Swaledale.

the woodland there is compensation, for the walking gets easier, and there are glimpses of high cliffs and scree above the ravine. The path turns right through a gap in the wall to head towards Keld. At a track junction **7** keep left, still with the Pennine Way, then just before reaching Keld, where fields appear to the left, turn sharp right **8** for the footbridge below the falls **A**.

This is a lovely spot to linger on the grassy bank by the falls and is a popular place for picnickers, a fact not lost on the local chaffinches that hop around at your feet collecting crumbs. The path leads on across the top of the falls and, in contrast to the walk on the opposite side of the valley, this is a broad track running across the face of the hill. The view, however, is not a jot less inspiring for the river splashes down its ravine bounded by sheer crags rising up through the trees. You enter an area of old mine workings where the path divides **9**. Here you leave the main track which is heading down to the valley floor and turn left onto a stony path heading round the hill towards Swinner Gill. It climbs up past old mining remains to pass above the sad dereliction that was once oddly named Crackpot Hall. Once clear of the spoil this becomes an absolutely delightful path, which is actually part of the Coast to Coast path and Wainwright who, of course, devised the route invites those who come this way to look with pity on the poor souls walking the far less agreeable Pennine Way. Certainly no one could complain about following this grassy path that runs round the hillside above the deep, rocky gill.

At the head of the valley, there are more old mining remains, where adits have been driven deep into the hillside beside the high waterfall **B**. Cross the stream on the bridge and turn left up the deep cleft to go between the ruined mine buildings. Now a rough path leads up the gill beside the stream which bounces along over falls high and low. A good, strenuous climb brings you to the top of the hill where the stream, now reduced to little more than a trickle, is crossed to reach a broad track. Go straight over onto a footpath way-marked by yellow-tipped posts. The typical peat and heather moorland is inevitably boggy in places, but firm ground is soon reached and a stony path leads up to the broad track where you turn right.

This track leads across a huge expanse of moor, and once you have crossed a little narrow gill, that is all you have in view – nothing but the moor and a steady swell of hills. The path climbs gently until you finally reach the top of the hill, the vista widens and you now look down into Swaledale. At the track junction **10** carry straight on passing traditional grouse butts, built as a horseshoe of drystone walling with a turf topping. Passing yet more old mine workings, the track now begins to swing right and head back towards the dale. Everything is still very open, the moor coloured by patches of heather. The track doubles round to cross a stream cascading down the valley, then turns to run along the rim of Gunnerside Gill.

Down below, the beck wriggles along the deep cleft until it is lost from sight among the trees. While the path remains very much on the moor, the opposite side of the gill is a mosaic of tiny fields. Where the main track starts to turn away in a sweeping bend to the right by a cairn **11** carry straight on along the grassy path heading down the rough hillside towards the houses. The path is not always very distinct, and can be boggy in places, but as long as you keep heading for the houses all will be well. There is a final brisk descent to the road that leads back to the centre of Gunnerside.

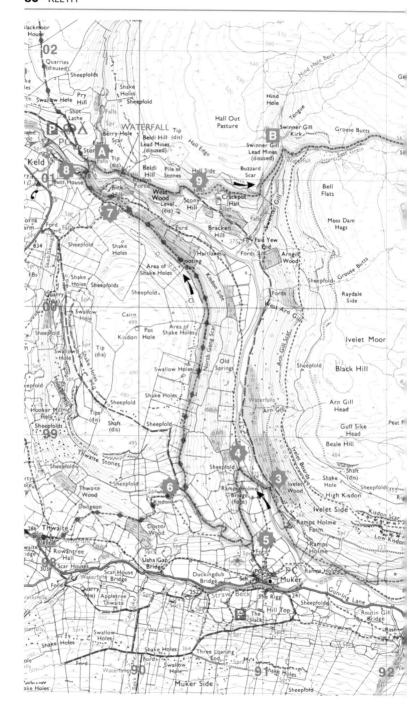

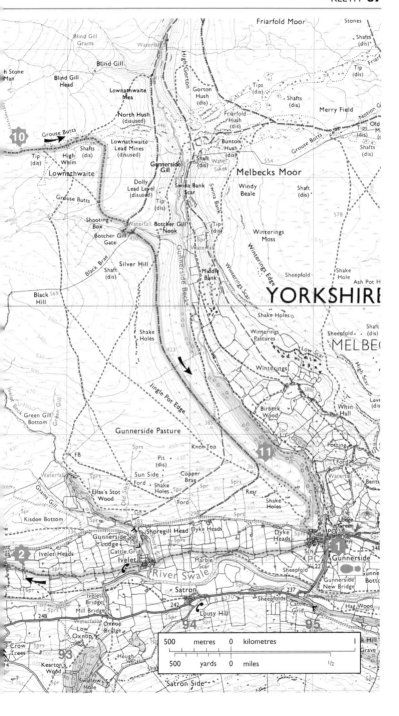

Friarfold Moor

Stones

Shafts (dis)

Blind Gill Grains

Waterfall

Blind Gill

High Gorton

Gorton Hush (dis)

Tips (dis)

Shafts (dis)

Merry Field

h Stone Man

Blind Gill Head

Lownathwaite Mea

Friarfold Hush (dis)

Shafts (dis)

Grouse Butts

North Hush (disused)

446

Bunton Hush (dis)

Grouse Butts

Shafts (dis)

10

Tip (dis)

High Whim

Shafts (dis)

Lownathwaite Lead Mines (disused)

Gunnerside Gill

Shaft (dis)

Water Sikes

Melbecks Moor

554

Lownathwaite

Dolly Lead Level (disused)

Swina Bank Scar

Swina Bank

Windy Beale

Shaft (dis)

Grouse Butts

Tip (dis)

578

Shooting Box

Waterfall

Botcher Gill Nook

Tip (dis)

Winterings Moss

570

Botcher Gill Gate

Black Brae

Silver Hill

Waterfall

Gunnerside Beck

Middle Bank

Winterings Edge

Sheepfold

Shake Hole

Ash Pot H

Black Hill

569

Shaft (dis)

YORKSHIRE

Shake Holes

Shaft (dis)

540

530

Shake Holes

423

Winterings Pastures

Winterings

Low Scar

Sheepfold

MELBE

High Scar

Shaft (dis)

Leve (dis)

500

Jingle Pot Edge

Birbeck Wood

Whin Hall

Green Gill Bottom

Green Gill

470

450

Gunnerside Pasture

386

Knot Top

Spr

38

11

Potting

(Ford)

Waterfall

Bents

FB

Pit (dis)

430

400

36

Sprs

Sun Side Ford

Shake Holes

Copper Brae

350

Resr

Shake Holes

Lodge Green

PC

Elias's Stot Wood

Ford

298

Sprs

Kisdon Bottom

Grains Gill

283

Shoregill Head

Dyke Heads

Dyke Heads

Spr

248

1

Gunnerside Lodge

Cattle Grid

220

2

Ivelet Heads

Ivelet

Marble Scar

Sheepfold

22

Sch PO

Gunnerside

Gunnerside Bott

River Swale

237

Gunnerside New Bridge

Satron

Hag Wood

Ivelet Bridge

Mill Bridge

242

Lousy Hill

Sheepfolds

Cattle Grid

94

95

248

Waterfalls

Low Oxnop

Oxnop Bridge

Hill Grave

Crow Trees

Kearton's Wood

93

Heugh

Swallow Hole

Satron Side

500	metres	0	kilometres	

500	yards	0	miles	1/2

The barren landscape of Swinner Gill boasts some of the wildest scenery in the Dales

Aysgarth

The village itself is best known for the falls which are actually some distance away, but are visited on Walk 1. But it has a character all its own, and is a very popular centre for the exploration of eastern Wensleydale on the fringe of the National Park.

WALK 1 — The Ure Valley and Bolton Castle

12 miles (19.5km) See map on pages 94 and 95

This is a very gentle walk by Dales standards, but one full of interest. The Ure valley is a delight, and not just because of the famous Aysgarth Falls, the countryside is always attractive and there is a chance to visit a grand medieval fortress.

Take the minor road that leads off the A 684 past the Methodist chapel. At the end of the road 1 cross the stile to join the little lane that leads out into the fields. A clear path leads via gates and stiles to a camp site and on to the road. Cross straight over and go up the drive to the church, an ancient foundation but almost entirely rebuilt by the Victorians. Carry on past the church on the path through the graveyard to continue the walk over the fields. The path leads through a little copse into humpy, undulating fields, to arrive above the wooded river valley to a roar of falling water. You come out by the lower falls **A**, dropping down over rock ledges, and as you pass above them you can look back at the river hammering down a rocky gorge. The excitement over, the river runs placidly for a while over the flat slabs of the bedrock. The path reaches the bank of the river where it is indulging in little flurries and dashes round rocks. A stile now leads to a pleasant waterside walk, but on reaching a small gate by a farm gate, you turn diagonally across the fields towards a patch of woodland. This brings you to the road **2** where you turn left to cross the bridge over Walden Beck and then immediately left again onto the path beside the beck. Go round the farm with the copse behind it and down across the field to rejoin the river.

The river, swollen and broadened by its tributary stream is now altogether more placid, lolloping along between grassy banks. There is now an obvious waterside path through the meadows. A curious domed tower can be seen on the hillside to the right, marking the preceptory of the Knights Templars. Anyone wishing to test their agility can try the stepping stones across the river, but the walk itself remains on this side. Once past the stones, the path climbs up through the woods to a stile which you cross to follow the path beside the trees. The walk now follows a narrow, steep-sided valley, with woodland across the water. A brief interlude of fields ends at more woodland, where once again you climb to the top of the bank, where you go through a gate and turn left along the edge of the wood. While all the walking here is very soft and gentle, the views to the right are of wilder country, dominated by the flat-topped hill of the Height of Hazely. Closer to hand, there is a gentle swell of grassland, dotted with splendid old trees. Eventually a gate leads into the wood, where there are still more grand, mature oak and beech. Once again the sound of rushing water is the prelude to the sight of a set of falls **B**, every bit as attractive as the more famous Aysgarth Falls and enhanced by the beautiful woodland setting. There is a viewpoint just before the path turns right to leave the woods.

The next part of the walk takes you through a remarkable landscape of limestone hummocks, like green sand dunes. The route follows the wall on the left, then turns away where the humps end to follow the foot of the rising ground to the right, while the river disappears round a wide, sweeping bend. Then, as the view opens out, you get an early sight of Bolton Castle, with its commanding position overlooking the valley. Once again the path returns to the river bank, and once again the landscape subtly changes. The walk is still over fields, but now a sprightly rabbit colony puts in an appearance. The view has opened out along the dale, with its gentle slopes to the north and higher hills to the south, while the river itself is now lined with trees. You catch a glimpse of a bridge up ahead and the path turns away from the river to a stile and a bridge across a stream **3** just past the wooded knoll. From here the path goes to the farthest corner of the field from the river, and continues across the middle of the next fields to meet a formal driveway **4**.

Turn left towards Bolton Hall **C** and after the long walk beside the Ure you finally get to cross the slow, deep river on an elegant bridge of two semicircular arches and prominent cut-waters. Follow the drive as it curves to the left towards Bolton Hall, an imposing rather than beautiful house, rather stolid with an array of terraces and balustrades. The approach is through typical parkland studded with trees. You arrive at a track junction **5** in front of the

The approach to Bolton Castle.

Hall where you turn left to take the track that runs along beside the wood. Eventually it enters the woodland as a pleasant grassy track through the trees with occasional glimpses of the river. Conifers give way to an area of mixed woodland, dominated by majestic oak. At the crossroads at the edge of the wood carry straight on to leave by the gate, and now you have a clear view of Bolton Castle **D**. The castle provides a most imposing marker as the path heads straight across the fields towards it. Passing a new barn you arrive at a lane and continue in the same direction, passing a little church on the right, and ending at the road at the edge of Redmire **6**.

Turn left towards the main road then right to the village centre with its green, where trees spread their branches wide for shady comfort. Turn left at the green and follow the road round to the right past the Bolton Arms. Just before reaching the high railway bridge, turn left **7** on the path between the houses and cross the fields via squeeze stiles to reach the beck, conveniently boulder-strewn for an easy crossing. Continue towards the castle with the stone wall to your left, and as you come through the wall turn slightly uphill to a squeeze stile and cross the track of the now disused railway. Continue diagonally uphill, still heading for the castle and now you can see just what a well chosen site it occupies. It has no very daunting natural defences, but with such immense views there would be time enough to prepare for an attack from any direction. From a squeeze stile, turn right through a gate to reach the road **8** where you turn left into Castle Bolton.

The village has a lovely, simple fourteenth-century church, but the castle itself is inevitably the dominant feature. No frivolity here: a grim, quadrilateral fortress with towers at each corner, it was built for Lord Scrope in 1378. Unlike many medieval fortresses it was not slighted by order of Cromwell at the end of the Civil War, though an order was made that it should remain unoccupied for 300 years. Today, fully restored, it is open to visitors. From the castle take the road heading back downhill, and where the road turns left **9** carry straight on along the bridleway. Where the track ends at the houses, cross the old railway once again and take the footpath that goes on a diagonal across the fields over a series of stiles to the road **10**. Turn right onto the road, which goes through a bend and begins to climb slightly. Turn left onto the footpath by the entrance to Sunny Bank Farm **11**, and where the track swings left, turn right towards the more distant farm. This brings you to a farm track where you turn left at the barns. Go through the gate, turn right through the farmyard and left through the gate – not as complex as it sounds. Now head diagonally across the next two fields to join a farm track heading down into the valley. It runs round in front of a farm, then turns left just before the outbuildings **12** to join the very clear track heading downhill towards the woodland. Head for a gate in the fence on the right beside a large clump of trees, and a gap in the thorn on the left brings you on the path down to the main Aysgarth Falls **E**.

The path wanders through the woodland, and there are turnings off for the various viewing points where visitors can enjoy the falls, which like the lower falls met earlier in the walk, cascade down over a series of ledges, where dippers hop about unconcerned by the foaming water all around them. The main path leads through coppiced hazel wood, dotted here and there by carved benches with suitably pastoral inscriptions. After visiting the falls, the path leads down to the road **13** where you turn left to the bridge and Yore Mill. This old water-powered mill has had a varied history, first built in 1784, rebuilt after a fire in 1850, its output included the red cloth that was used for the famous red shirts of Garibaldi's army. Today it houses a carriage museum. The road now climbs steeply up towards the church where you turn right, back through the campsite to retrace your steps to the village.

WALK 2	Bishopdale and West Burton
	11.5 miles (18.5km) See map on pages 100 and 101

This walk involves a steady climb to the hills above Wensleydale, with a visit to an important prehistoric monument, followed by a visit to Bishopdale and an attractive finish down the Walden valley.

Start from the village centre by taking the minor road that leads off the A 684 towards Thornton Rust. Once clear of the houses, this becomes a peaceful country lane with a view down to the river winding its way down Wensleydale. Where the road turns right **1** by an isolated barn, turn left on the bridleway to Gayle Ing. The track soon swings right and now you can see it as a continuous line snaking up the hillside. At the track junction **2** turn right, and you go through a mixed landscape, alternating between good, rich grassland divided up into small fields and the larger units of rough pasture. The result is a subtle patchwork of darker greens, shading into the paler shades and russets of the moorland. You carry straight on to a point where a footpath crosses the line of the track. After passing this field and the next on the left, look out for the stile which gives you access to Castle Dykes henge **A**. This is a classic neolithic henge with bank and ditch forming an oval enclosure – but with no standing stones. Walk up to what looks at first like a mound in the middle of the field, but which turns out to be the bank rising above a reed-filled ditch. It is well worth the diversion, if only for the chance to pause and conjecture why people built this monument in such a lonely spot some 4000 years ago.

Return to the track to continue on your way, and there is a brief interruption to the steady uphill progress as you drop down to ford a little stream. Now stony outcrops begin to appear, and it is worth stopping to look back onto the ring of the henge and out beyond it to Bolton Castle. Where the way divides **3** turn left beside the little stream, which may well be dried up in summer, and cross it to go through the gap in the wall. Continue up with the wall on your right, on what is now a grassy track over the rough moor. As the walls are left behind, simply continue straight on along the well defined path heading up to the ridge. This is real, lonely upland where curlews cry, but little else breaks the silence. Coming up over the ridge, the hills rise up ahead of you, while immediately in front the land falls away to a hollow where a farm sits snugly in a protective arc of trees. The track leads on to a ruined barn and a stile, with a footpath signposted to Thoralby. Take the path to the left of the trees and then, topping a little rise, follow it down to a footbridge. This is a lovely little valley with its busy stream, a pleasant spot to linger before taking the steep little climb up the other side to a clear path that swings round to the left through a mass of heather to reach a rutted track **4**.

Turn left onto this track which soon becomes a wide, grassy path running along a ridge with views down to Wensleydale on one side and Bishopdale on the other. Soon it begins to head downhill to the village of Thoralby. The track heads straight down between hills patched with woodland to the road **5** where you turn left. This is in many ways a typical Dales street, with a profusion of seventeenth-century houses, many with traditional mullioned windows but, more unusually, a number of round headed windows as well. On reaching the triangular green **6** turn right at the T-junction for the road that winds steeply downhill. An old corn mill, now converted, stands by the bridge over Bishopdale Beck, beyond which you turn right towards Kettlewell. Cross straight over the main road towards Newbiggin.

At the T-junction at the top of the hill **7** turn left onto the road that soon peters out to a rough track. Where the track divides keep straight on up the hill towards a gate, and now the little lane opens out, and you turn to follow the wall on the left to cross the foot of the little gully. The path continues diagonally across the face of the hill, with views down Bishopdale to the wide, flat valley bottom of Wensleydale. Reaching a wall, with a patch of silver birch behind it **8**, turn right up the hill towards the conifers. Carry on up with the trees to your left and the wall on the right and turn right to follow the edge of the plantation. The path levels out and you reach a stile in the fence **9** where you turn left onto the forest track. This is a typical conifer plantation, with trees packed together in gloomy ranks, but the pine needles provide a cushioned path underfoot. The track ends at a rather daunting clearing with waist high ferns, and no very obvious path. Strike out boldly through the undergrowth, still walking in the same direction, at an angle from the wall and you will soon see a gap in the trees up ahead and a stile leading back into the wood. Forest tracks can be wide rutted thoroughfares, but this is a genuinely peaceful footpath. Cross a small clearing to a final little wriggly path that turns left to a stile leading out to the road **10**.

Turn right up the road and you are now walking up the very beautiful Walden valley with moorland rising steeply at the head.

The broad village green at West Burton, with its border of traditional stone houses.

The road doubles round to cross a stream, and as you climb up from the bridge turn left on the footpath for Cote Bridge **11**. The land seems very rich which is no surprise, for it sits between Wensleydale and Coverdale both noted for their dairy herds and cheeses. Where the track divides you head left towards the farm. Just before reaching the farmhouse itself, turn left round the out-buildings to reach a footbridge over the stream. There is now an obvious path, but coming out into the open do not cross the stile directly ahead, but follow the footpath diversion. Turn right along the fence towards the valley floor and then follow it round to the left – going round the field rather than straight across it. Now the way ahead is absolutely straightforward, crossing a whole succession of fields with the river down to your right. On the map it may look like a familiar type of Dales walk through a succession of hay meadows, but in practice it is a quite extraordinarily diverse route. There are hay fields, but these alternate with others of rough, coarse grass and these, in turn, give way to others where the path heads through ferns that in midsummer can grow to shoulder height. And all the time you have the rock-faced hills around you. As you reach the lower valley, so the ground becomes richer and the fields narrower, so that you find yourself constantly passing through squeeze stiles which, like the fields, seem to shrink and get ever squeezier. This delightful route then finds a new variation, running above a wood where the greenery is enlivened by splashes of red rowan berries and the pale streaks of silver birch.

Reaching a large field after a succession of narrow ones, with buildings on the far side, turn right towards the bridge. One last stile now brings you to the road **12**. Turn right to cross the beck, then immediately left through the gate to join the path at the water's edge. The beck bowls along cheerfully under a canopy of trees and you stay with it to the footbridge which you cross to continue on the opposite bank. The path then turns up past the power line support to reach the road **13** where you turn right and then almost immediately left onto the path to Town Head. At the road turn right down to West Burton and its wide village green **B**. It is a good place to pause and explore and has one curious feature, an obelisk-like cross erected in the nineteenth century, and a splendid natural feature in the shape of the falls at the bottom end of the village.

Carry on down the main street beside the green, past the falls, which can be seen from a path leading to a footbridge on the right. After that diversion continue on the road to Burton Bridge and carry straight on along the B 6160. At the road junction **14** turn left onto the pavement by the pleasant tree-shaded Aysgarth road, and where the pavement ends hop over the little stile to continue on the grass. Rejoin the road to cross the bridge, and once across where the main road swings right **15** carry straight on along the very narrow minor road. Where that turns sharp left go straight on across the field with the wall on your left to a stile and then climb the hill up to the barn. Pass to the left of the building and go up the field past a little line of conifers. Immediately beyond them, look out for a footpath sign on the left and a stile which you cross to continue in the same direction heading down into the valley. At the path junction carry straight on and coming up out of a dip, cross the stile in the wall on the right and head across the field on a diagonal to a signpost on the skyline. Cross straight over the road and over the next field, then cut across the corner to the left for the path down to the road **16**. Turn right down to the main road, then left to return to the centre of Aysgarth.

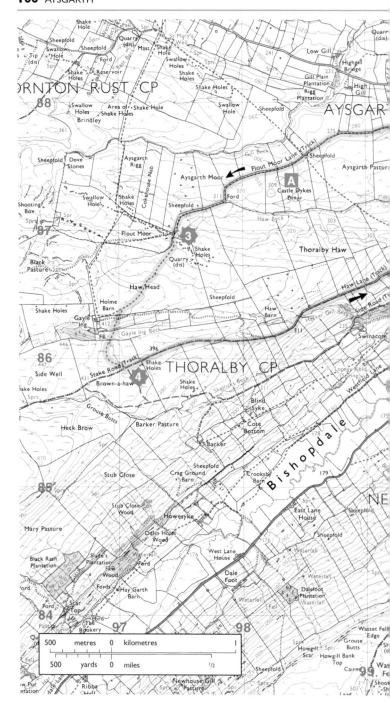

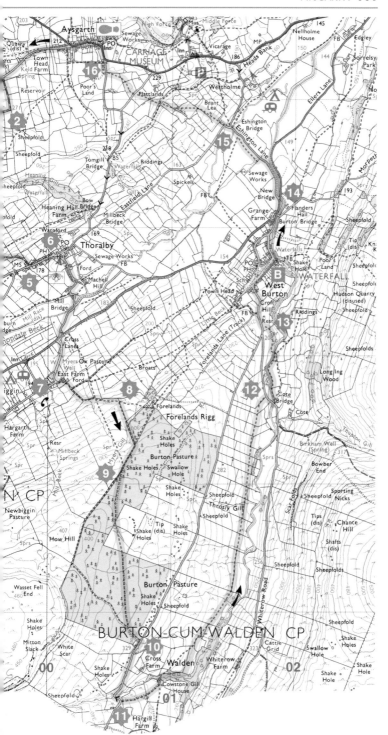

A magnificent panorama seen from the great circular bank and ditch of the neolithic

henge.

Kettlewell

One of the most attractive spots in Wharfedale, and a good deal quieter than more touristy Grassington just down the road. With its youth hostel, inns and B and Bs there is no problem with accommodation, and its riverside site makes it an ideal place to relax at the end of a good day's walking.

WALK 1 Hubberholme and Buckden Pike

12 miles (20km) See map on pages 108 and 109

After a gentle start, following the Dales Way beside the river, the walk climbs to the plateau above the charming village of Hubberholme and returns via the 2303 feet (702 metre) summit of Buckden Pike.

Leave Kettlewell by taking the B 6160 Burnsall road to cross the bridge 1. Turn right through the gate, and immediately turn off the broad track to drop down to the riverside path. All of the next section, as far as Hubberholme, follows the splendid long-distance path, the Dales Way. Soon the path moves away from the bank to join a stony lane running between stone walls. This is a very fertile valley, liberally speckled with woodland. Many of the fields have been kept as traditional hay meadows, seen at their best in late spring and early summer when the air is heavy with the scent of flowers and herbs, where after harvest time you are more likely to encounter the less agreeable aroma of silage. The route is very easy to follow over the fields and the Wharfe is never far away with its varied bird life, from the statuesque heron to the bustling oyster catchers with their sharp, piping cries.

Continuing past the footbridge to Starbotton, you arrive at a particularly attractive stretch of river, shaded by sycamore and ash. Then the river turns away, leaving behind a broad swathe of marsh. The path keeps clear and dry at the foot of the hill, with its attractive covering of broad-leaved woodland, through which the occasional fir spires up to the sky. A footbridge across a stream brings you into National Trust land and a lane where your shoulders brush against tall foxgloves and cow parsley, and the fields to either side are especially rich with flowers. The path comes up to and runs through the fringe of what is really a very grand section of woodland, with sudden startling bursts of colour produced by bronzed copper beech. After this brief but very pleasant interlude the path turns back to the river, now heading towards Buckden. Cross the road by the double-arched bridge at Buckden to continue on the path by the water, still staying on the same side of the river. Now the river seems positively sluggish, a lazy brown drift beneath the dipping branches of the trees. A stony path leads to a broader track that swings away from the river to reach the road on the outskirts of Hubberholme **2**.

Turn right up the road, passing the ivy covered manor, to the George Inn. Here you finally cross the river to reach the church **A**. This may not be the grandest church in the Dales, but it is surely the most delightful with its elaborate screen and rare rood loft, its lovely old timber roof and no less attractive modern pews by Robert Thompson, who has left his carved mouse mark on each. The path passes to the right of the church to join the broad track leading up the hill to Scar House. The house itself has the date of 1698 over the door, but was sympathetically rebuilt in 1876. Once past the house **3** turn right on the footpath to Cray. There is a little scramble up through the rocks of the scar itself to the top of the hill and the grass path above the woods. You now come out onto a broad terrace of springy turf with a limestone pavement at the valley rim. At a break in the trees, where a thorn bush has managed to find a solitary home in among the rock, you can look out down Wharfedale over the route you have just walked.

This section of the walk is a real delight, but its character changes on reaching a deep gully, which is crossed on a footbridge. Once across, a rougher path is followed which soon swings away from the stream to run through fields. It is something of a surprise to find hay meadows at this height, over 1000 feet (350 metres). The path cuts across to join the farm track leading down to the road by the White Lion Inn **4**. Cross straight over the road and use the stepping stones to cross the stream. Once across, follow the wall to climb straight up the hill to reach another soft, green track **5** where you turn right. After a quarter of a mile, just before reaching a gate, turn back to the left **6** to take the path heading on a long diagonal slope up the hill and signposted to Buckden Pike.

It looks an encouragingly easy slope and the top seems not to be very far away: it is all deception. The slope steepens and you reach an area of peat moorland which, as is invariably the case, has its fair share of boggy patches. And, like so many rounded hills, each summit is a fake, which as soon as you reach it only reveals the next climb. The final section runs up beside the stone wall to reach the trig point **B** from where you can look out over Wharfedale to the distant Three Peaks, a view which makes all the effort worth while. From here, cross the ladder stile and turn right along the line of the wall. At first the going is easy, then the bogs set in, but you can find an easier, drier route by moving some 20-30 yards away from the wall. Eventually you arrive at the monument to the Polish airmen who lost their lives in the Second World War **C**.

Continue following the wall to the end, then go through the gate on the right **7** to head downhill towards the deep vee of the gill leading down to Starbotton. Just before reaching the point where a long stone wall runs across the path, just above the head of the gill, turn left by a cairn **8** onto a faint path heading across the moor towards a gate. Once again this is somewhat boggy, as you would expect seeing so much cotton grass around, and the path goes through a squelchy area of springs. But this is short lived and soon a drier path leads on to an area of spoil heaps. Make your way across the head of a rock strewn gully and take the path past the cairn for a walk along the rim of the valley, much more comfortable now and enjoying excellent views out over Wharfedale. The clear path eventually reaches the long wall sweeping across the head of the valley and there is a pleasant grassy path running between the wall and the escarpment.

Where the tracks divide **9** turn right to head downhill to a T-junction of tracks where you turn left. At the next junction **10** you turn sharp right for the descent to Kettlewell. Stony at first, this gives way to a more comfortable grass path, still with tremendous views. The track runs down one side of a deep gill and across the other side you can see a crazy paving effect of fields, one of which is bizarrely totally enclosed by another. It contrasts with the valley floor laid out in a neat pattern of uniform stripes. Kettlewell itself remains hidden from view until you are practically on top of it, and then a rough and very steep descent brings you down to the road where you turn right for the village centre.

Looking along Wharfedale from the lane that leads back to Kettlewell at the end of the walk.

WALK 2	Hebden and Grassington

11 miles (18km) See map on pages 114 and 115

A walk of contrasts, which starts with a deep gorge, crosses the moors to one of the best preserved lead mining sites in the area and returns via riverside and hills – a bit of everything.

Start at the little village of Conistone, 3 miles (5km) from Kettlewell down a minor road. This is a neat, compact village with a triangular green and Norman church. The walk itself begins at the T-Junction **1** by the green, where you take the little road heading past the old schoolhouse towards the hillside. The road carries straight on as a track between the houses at the end of which you go through a gate for the path up the hill. It is tempting not to say what happens next, because it comes as such a wonderful surprise. As you climb, there is a little scramble up rocks and you reach what it quite clearly the dried up bed of a stream that once ran down a deep gorge – it is like a smaller scale Gordale Scar without the water **A**. As you climb, so the rock walls close in rising sheer to either side. A bend in the gorge must have sent the water shooting down against the rock face opposite, where it scooped out a great hollow. On the next section the rock walls are so close together that standing between them you can put a hand on each face. You emerge from the gorge to a narrow valley between scree-covered slopes. The gradient eases and walking is comfortable on a broad, grass track that runs though convoluted hills which look as if they have been deliberately and neatly folded.

Where the track divides **2** continue straight on to the next of the clefts and another dried-up stream bed tumbling down through the cliffs. Cross a ladder stile, and now there is a short scramble up what must once have been an attractive waterfall. A second ladder stile **3** brings you out to a wide track, actually part of the Dales Way, where you turn left to reach a track junction at which you turn right. This is very much limestone country, with an extensive pavement above the scar edge and a lime kiln built into the hillside. At the next track junction **4** turn right and now you get extensive views out over Wharfedale and crag-edged Kilnsey Moor. Beyond a ladder stile, the track swings round to the left heading gently uphill to the top of the moor.

At the summit, a wall comes in from the right **5** and you leave the main track to follow it, then cross through so that the wall is now on your left. At the shake hole, by a length of wooden fencing, you turn slightly away from the wall on to a bright green path running through the pallid moorland grasses. Route finding is slightly difficult as walls have tumbled where once there were stiles and gates. However, there is a landmark to aim for on the hill up ahead of you where you can see two cairns on the skyline, and you aim for the one in the middle of the hill. Another indicator is a tall, solitary chimney which is slightly to the left of the line of the wall. Your compass should also should also reassure you that you are heading almost due south. In any case, as you continue the path becomes more distinct, passing though coarse grass and thistles. Conformation of the route soon appears in the form of a ladder stile. It is still very fine upland country, completely surrounded by hills and passing though an area of shake holes.

Reaching a little knoll, you go through the left hand of two gates to join a lane between stone walls. At the end of this lane continue, as shown by an arrow, by heading towards a wall on the right to join the obvious rutted track. This leads on past appropriately named High Barn, now a sad ruin. The wall on the left has incorporated boulders simply left in situ and beyond that there is a wide expanse of heather. Rounding a bend, you come on to the heaps of stone rubble that tell you that you are back in mining country, and there are now houses in sight in front of you. Leave the main track by the gate on the right **6** and take the path down past the houses to the road and cross straight over onto the bridleway.

Now the walk enters one of the most important lead mining areas in the region. Deep mining involved huge capital expenditure for sinking shafts, draining them by adits which burrowed deep into the hills to carry away the water from the workings as well as the actual costs of extracting and processing the ore. Here the money for development in the eighteenth century was supplied by the Duke of Devonshire, hence the name 'Dukes's New Road' on the map. As you walk past the spoil heaps you can also see bell pits. These were once shallow bell shaped shafts with the spoil heaped around them in a ring, and when they collapsed they left the typical doughnut shape. The little lake was a reservoir which provided water for the water-wheels that powered ore-crushing machinery, and just beyond that is the main mining area **B**. It is well worth exploring and there are numbered plaques explaining what is what. By number 10, if you go through a low archway into a dripping tunnel you can peer straight down a 360-foot (110-metre) shaft fenced off for safety. The chimney on the hill stands above the old smelting cupola.

The beautiful, tree-shaded River Wharfe as seen from the walk near Linton.

From the site make your way to the gate with a small building behind it and take the path round to the left to the Hebden Beck which is now followed back towards Wharfedale. This is a very attractive valley with bracken-covered hills above the busy stream, but signs of mining are never far away. Where the wide track crosses the stream, for example, you can see the arched entrance to an old adit on the left **C**. The limestone has now been left behind for gritstone which appears in the typical outcrops of big, square blocks. A bridge crosses back over the gill **7** where the water rushes down over falls and the path ends to continue as a surfaced road that runs down the edge of the gill into Hebden.

Cross straight over the main road and take the road opposite signposted to Burnsall. Pass the old village school, now a tea room, and at the foot of the hill **8** turn right towards the suspension bridge over the Wharfe. Do not cross the bridge but turn right onto the riverside walk and you are back once again on the Dales

Way. This is all very delightful; the river is broad and gentle, the path smooth and grassy and the way shaded by a parade of trees including magnificent horse chestnut. Then the path runs through woodland and when it emerges path and river diverge, and you head across to a footbridge over a stream before rejoining the river bank. Here a rush of water announces the arrival at Linton Falls – one natural waterfall and two weirs built to supply water for a woollen mill now demolished. Now the path turns away to the road bridge and its heavily buttressed causeway.

Cross straight over the road to the right of the bridge **9** and continue on the footpath to Wood Lane. If you want to visit Grassington itself, turn right up the main road then left up the High Street to the Town Hall, then left down Chapel Street to rejoin the walk at **10**. Meanwhile, the main route leads up between the houses. Cross the road and go up the steps. Cross over the next road to Moody Sty which leads to Garrs End Lane where you turn left. Follow the road round uphill to the right to reach a splendid seventeenth-century farmhouse **10** where you turn left on the footpath to Conistone.

Once through the farmyard and out on the fell side you are confronted by three gateways. Take the middle one and cross the field entering an area of humps and hollows, all that remains of a medieval village. Where the path divides **11** cross a stile and turn left towards the wood. Now you reach an extensive area of limestone pavement and you continue across it with the wood to the left. Where the woodland boundary turns away downhill, just before the limestone escarpment comes to an end, look for a ladder stile by a gate on the left **12**. Once across it, turn right to a squeeze stile then right again onto the path that winds very steeply down the slope. Cross over the head of the deep cleft by a stone stile and turn left along the path beside the wall. It may not be quite as dramatic as the gill up from Conistone, but it runs it a close second with tall cliffs rising sheer up the sides. Now the path emerges as a clear, grassy way through bracken with a wall to the left. You come down to a ferny bowl beneath the crags and now the dark shape of Kilnsey Crag glowers out across the valley. The final descent is through meadows and back down to the Wharfe and, if you see them when they are at their best, you will find a wealth of flowers from the common buttercup to the exotic orchid. The field path ends at a farm track which leads down to the road **13** where you turn right past a fine seventeenth-century stone house to return to the centre of Conistone.

The landscape of mining: the remains of an old bell pit on the moors above Grassing

USEFUL INFORMATION

ACCOMMODATION IN THE YORKSHIRE DALES

The National Park Authority publishes a free information newspaper annually, *The Yorkshire Dales Visitor* and this gives useful advice on all aspects of the park including accommodation. Tourist Information centres for the park can also be contacted or one of the many bed and breakfast guides can be consulted. The YHA has a number of hostels in the area and can be contacted at Trevelyan House, 8 St Stephens Hill, St Albans, Herts AL1 2DY (tel: 01727 855215).

Youth Hostels
Aysgarth Falls: Leyburn DL8 3SR (tel: 01969 663260) GR 98/ 102884

Dentdale: Cowgill, Sedbergh LA10 5RN (tel: 01539 625251) GR 98/ 773850

Grinton Lodge: Grinton, Richmond DL11 6HS (tel: 01748 884206) GR 98/ 048975

Hawes: Lancaster Terrace, Hawes DL8 3LQ, (tel: 01969 667368) GR 98/ 867897

Ingleton: Greta Tower, Sammy Lane, Ingleton, Carnforth LA6 3EG; (tel: 01524 241444); GR 98/ 695733

Keld: Keld Lodge, Upper Swaledale, Richmond DL11 6LL (tel: 01748 886259) GR 91/ 891009

Kettlewell: Whernside House, Kettlewell, Skipton BD23 5QU (tel: 01756 760232) GR 98/ 970724

Linton: The Old Rectory, Linton-in-Craven, Skipton BD23 5HH (tel: 01756 752400) GR 98/ 998627

Malham: John Dower Memorial Hostel, Malham, Skipton BD23 4DE (tel: 01729 830321) GR98/ 901629

Stainforth: 'Taitlands', Stainforth, Settle BD24 9PA (tel: 01729 823577) GR 98/ 821668

Tourist information Centres

Aysgarth: Aysgarth Falls, National Park Centre, Leyburn
DL8 3TH (tel: 01969 663424) (S)

Grassington: National Park Centre, Colvend, Hebden Road,
Grassington BD23 5LB (tel: 01756 752774) (S)

Hawes: Dales Countryside Museum, Station Yard, Hawes
DL8 3NT (tel: 01969 667450)

Ingleton: The Community Centre, Ingleton, LA63 3HG
(tel: 01524 241049) (S)

Malham: National Park Centre, Malham, Skipton BD23 4DA
(tel: 01729 830363)

Reeth: The Literary Institute, The Green, Reeth DL11 6TE
(tel: 01748 884059)

Sedbergh: 72 Main Street, Sedbergh LA10 5AD
(tel: 01539 620125) (S)

Settle: Town Hall, Cheapside, Settle BD24 9EJ (tel: 01729 825192)

Horton-in-Ribblesdale: Pen-y-Ghent Café, Horton-in-
Ribblesdale BD24 0HE (tel: 01729 860333)

Leyburn: 4 Central Chambers, Market Place, Leyburn DL8 5BB
(tel: 01969 623069)

(S) Seasonal April to October

Yorkshire Dales National Park

Headquarters: National Park Centre, Colvend, Hebden Road,
Grassington BD23 5LB (tel: 01756 752774)

Clapham via Lancaster LA28 8ED (tel: 015242 51419)

Malham: Malham, Skipton BD23 4DA (tel: 01729 830363)

The centres at Aysgarth, Hawes, Reeth and Sedbergh are at the
same address as the tourist information centre.

Local Weather Reports:
Meteorological Office Weathercall

North East England 0906 8500418

Ordnance Survey Maps

Outdoor Leisure Maps 1:25,000 2, 19, 30

Landranger Maps 1: 50,000 92, 97, 98, 99, 103